Praise for *FPL Obsessed: Tips for Success in Fantasy Premier League*

"A good read for those who are just starting with the game as well as those who have obsessed over it for years."

Pranil Sheth (Lateriser12)
Writer for *Fantasy Football Scout* and Co-host of *The FPL Wire*

"This was such an easy and enjoyable read... I finished the book in a matter of days! I found myself relating to much of what I read whilst also picking up some fantastic tips along the way. This book sits proudly on the FPL JUiCE studio desk and has done since I finished it!"

Ash – FPL JUiCE
Co-host of *FPL JUiCE* Podcast

"A great read! I am looking forward to the next edition."

FPL Focal
Former FPL #1 and YouTuber

"Brilliant! As an FPL manager myself, this book really resonates. I enjoyed how Matt takes us through his years as an FPL manager. His anecdotes are funny and relatable and I feel like I know him better after reading the book."

KT – Fantasy Football Titan
Fantasy Football Scout International

"Wow! I honestly couldn't put this book down. It is a breath of fresh air."

Dan Lison
Founder of *The FPL Way*

FPL OBSESSED:

TIPS FOR SUCCESS IN FANTASY PREMIER LEAGUE

MATT WHELAN

Second Edition

First Edition published May 2021

Cover design by: Digitalian

Illustrations by: Jeremy Wise (FPL Doodles)

ISBN (paperback): 978-1-8384751-2-3

ISBN (ebook): 978-1-8384751-3-0

ISBN (hardcover): 978-1-8384751-8-5

Published by Arrowcroft Press

ARROWCROFT PRESS

This book is dedicated to every single FPL manager out there; for contributing towards the enjoyment of my favourite hobby.

CONTENTS

PREFACE

Fantasy Premier League (FPL) is an online game which attracts over eight million people each year, and the number is growing.

FPL puts players (or "managers") in charge of an imaginary budget of £100 million, which they must spend on 15 players who play in the English Premier League (EPL). Every week, when the matches are played, FPL managers earn points for their players based on their performance on the football field. When the season ends, the FPL manager with the most points overall wins.

The game's origins date back to 1963 when Wilfred "Bill" Winkenbach, part-owner of the Oakland Raiders American football team, along with some others, founded the Greater Oakland Professional Pigskin Prognosticators League, or GOPPPL for short. They had created the very first fantasy football game. GOPPPL had most of the current rules and format, head-to-head leagues, substitutions and Friday afternoon deadlines.

In the early 90s, fantasy football came to Europe when Riccardo Albini developed Fantacalcio (Italian Fantasy Football). It arrived in England shortly after, in 1991, when Andrew Wainstein created Fantasy League Ltd.

The *Daily Telegraph* launched their game, along with Wainstein, ahead of the 1993/94 season. Back then, players had to use premium rate telephone numbers, or the post, to make their changes prior to the Friday deadline.

While the game was already going online in the US, it was only in the 2000/01 season that the fantasy football world received an online presence in England, when fantasyleague.com launched their first online game.

Many other online versions followed, but it wasn't until the 2002/03 season that the Official Fantasy Premier League was launched. In that year, just under 76,000 players took part.

FPL was born.

NOTES ON SECOND EDITION

When this book was released in May 2021, I was overwhelmed by the support it received from the FPL community. When the reviews and messages from my readers started pouring in, I was completely blown away by the response the book was getting. I fully expected that once the season kicked off, sales of my book would diminish – but they did not. In fact, with each passing month, more and more copies were being purchased and, on multiple occasions, it was ranked as the #1 Amazon Best Seller in various categories.

I decided during the 2021/22 campaign that in early 2022, when the season was drawing to a close, I would update this book to a Second Edition. The reason for this came in two parts:

First, FPL is a game of constant learning. Successful managers must adapt to each new season and be prepared to revise their thinking. They must have the mental fortitude to admit when the tried-and-tested methods of the past are no longer relevant and have the humility to explore new paths. There is not a single season which has gone by where I have not discovered something new. Creating a Second Edition therefore is a way of ensuring the continuity of my ever-evolving thought processes as well as giving me an opportunity to share any new and exciting FPL resources which emerge each season.

Second, I wanted to keep the book fresh. Each passing season brings new highlights, low points and discussion topics. I didn't want to produce a book which, in a few years' time, feels outdated because it only refers to incidents long forgotten. With this Second Edition, I've been able to draw examples and anecdotes from the latest season while keeping the core philosophy of the book intact. It also gave me the opportunity to add all the things which I kicked myself, soon after publication, for leaving out in the first place!

Amongst other topics, here's a sample of some of the updated content which can be found in the Second Edition:

- Getting a low ID
- Disgruntled players in pre-season
- Taking note of your first proper draft
- The importance of identifying the exceptions to your own rules
- Not avoiding FPL assets just because they play for rival teams
- Does focusing on mini-leagues affect your overall rank?
- The "planned transfers" debate
- Using your Wildcard to capture player value
- How to create your own chip strategy in five easy steps
- Navigating Covid outbreaks
- Introducing my favourite stat (NPxG+xA/90)
- Why you shouldn't be too disheartened by a poor start
- How to get around the early kick-off captaincy dilemma.

I hope you enjoy reading this Second Edition as much as I have enjoyed writing it.

INTRODUCTION

It is 23rd January 2020 and Fantasy Premier League managers all over the world have been eagerly, and anxiously, awaiting this game. Wolves play Liverpool at Molineux. Liverpool have been utterly dominant in a season in which they will be crowned Premier League champions. In particular, Mo Salah and Sadio Mané have been in excellent form; so much so that many managers, myself included, have made sacrifices elsewhere in their teams to accommodate both these premium midfielders.

But there is something special about this Gameweek: it is one of the very few double Gameweeks of the season. A double Gameweek (DGW) can be an absolute game changer in terms of a manager's overall rank, or position in their own mini-leagues.

Over a million managers have given Mané the captain's armband, and just shy of 950,000 have given it to Salah. In addition, almost half a million managers have played their Triple Captain chip this week. I am one of them.

Weeks of painful deliberation have led to this moment. The stats and form between the two players are so close they are almost negligible. You may as well toss a coin. I went with Mané.

After 33 minutes, he picks up an injury and is taken off. His injury is sufficiently severe that he also misses the second match in the same double Gameweek. My reward for saving my Triple Captain until this point? Three measly points. Salah finished the double Gameweek with 16 points. Anyone who used their Triple Captain on Salah was rewarded with 48 points. There were always going to be winners and losers in the captaincy decision but nobody could have foreseen a difference of 45 points between the two players.

That decision, amongst other things, contributed to my overall rank tumbling to about 500k when I had been at 175k only a couple of weeks before. It also paved the way to the eventual victory of my mini-league nemesis, Dan,[1] who gave the armband to The Egyptian King.

The FPL Gods are cruel indeed.

***

Rewind a decade and twenty-five-year-old me is sitting in a party hostel called *The Wild Rover* in La Paz, Bolivia. My (now) wife and I were fortunate enough to take a year out from the Rat Race to travel the world for a year.

As I wait for Happy Hour to kick off, I log into my FPL account, using a dusty, beat-up PC which I have to pay £1 an hour (equivalent to a three-course meal out there) to use. When my Points screen loads, I am overjoyed to see that both Charlie Adam and Andy Carroll have double-digit returns for newly promoted Blackpool and Newcastle United respectively. Back in those days, FPL priced the newly promoted players too low. I was one of the few who had taken a punt on both players and was handsomely rewarded for it.

At this early stage of the season, I was catapulted into the higher rankings and was out of sight in all my mini-leagues. At the end of that season, I attained my best overall rank: 2,489th in the world. A few weeks before the end of the season, I was 275th in

[1] We'll get to *him* later.

the global rankings. I could scroll down from the top of the overall league and find my name in no time at all.

The FPL Gods were smiling on me that season.

WHAT IS THIS BOOK ABOUT?

The above story highlights the polarised nature of FPL. It can bring immense joy and crushing sadness. Non-casual FPL managers will already know exactly what I am talking about. If you are reading this book having recently started playing the game, trust me, you have a lot of mixed emotions to come.

Not everyone gets hooked on FPL. Many who play the game, and do not really care much for it, will lose interest at the inevitable point when they have a few consecutive low-scoring Gameweeks. They realise it isn't all fun and roses and will either stop taking it seriously or stop playing all together.

People who *are* serious about FPL will drag themselves through the painful Gameweeks, desperate to get to the other side. This commitment is what separates the FPL achievers from the ones who end up somewhere in the bottom half of the global rankings. Commitment alone, however, is not enough to consistently reach the upper echelons. You must have discipline, focus and willpower. These traits are immensely difficult to employ when your team is in an awful place and your rivals are leaving you for dust.

This book recognises that there are many different routes to success in FPL. Your own playing style is likely to be governed by how you gain enjoyment from the game. If you are relatively new to the game, there's a good chance that you are not yet aware what your own playing style is. This is therefore not a step-by-step guide on how to play FPL because you, as an individual, must decide how to play the game. Playing someone else's way won't work for you and, even if it did, it would sap the fun from the game.

Instead, this book draws from my 18 years' experience playing FPL to highlight common successful traits which transcend a multitude of playing styles. It will teach you how to master your own emotions, to resist the dark temptations available when things look bad, and how to make the right decisions for the long term, rather than constantly chasing short-term gains.

***

This book is divided into four parts:

Part One: Pre-Season deals with everything you should be doing from the moment the previous season ends, right up until the GW1 deadline of the next season. It covers all the important aspects of creating your initial squad.

Part Two: The Gameweeks covers everything from GW1 to GW38 and includes transfers, captaincy decisions, chip strategy and how to define and pursue your objectives for the season.

Part Three: Playing Styles explores the different playing styles commonly found amongst FPL managers and the merits and pitfalls of these different types of management.

Part Four: Psychology is all about the psychological aspects of playing FPL. This section emphasises the importance of enjoying the game and developing strategies for staying calm and focused when things are going badly.

WHO IS THIS BOOK FOR?

This book is for anyone with a bit more than a passing interest in FPL, and the fact you have bought it instantly qualifies you as having more than a passing interest.

I did not write this book for those who have never played the game before, so do not expect an explanation of the very basic mechanics of the game (although there is a Glossary of terms included at the back of the book for those who are unfamiliar with some of the terminology). But if you are hooked on the game and want to improve, then this book can help.

- Are you a relatively new manager who wants the edge to get ahead in your mini-leagues?
- Are you a veteran of the game still chasing your first Top 10k finish?
- Are you a content creator or high achiever who is trying to drown out the noise of the online FPL community and regain a bit of clarity?

It is not just about success; many managers have sadly forgotten how to enjoy the game. This could be because they are chasing a goal which evades them each season or, having achieved a string of high finishes, have gone backwards and can't seem to get back to winning ways. For these people, the pressure and disappointment of FPL can be immense and can even have a negative impact on their mental health and other aspects of their life.

A lot of what you are about to read may simply be me telling you what you already know deep down, but have maybe lost sight of while trying to navigate the relentless, and almost infinite, stream of contradicting opinions and advice out there.

If you can identify with any of the above, then this book is for you.

WHY SHOULD YOU LISTEN TO ME?

Most people will, understandably, want to head straight for a person's credentials before taking their advice, so here is a little bit about me.

First, I am a huge Liverpool fan and have been a supporter of my team since I was about five years old. My parents were never interested in football, so my uncle, Steve, got involved and bought me an LFC leather match ball signed by the entire squad of 1987/88.

Football has been a major part of my life ever since and I am now fortunate enough to share that same passion with my own children. I also run weekly football coaching sessions for young kids who live in my area but don't have the confidence to join the local teams.

I started playing FPL back in 2004 when an old school friend of mine, Pat Best, created a mini-league called *Hogs of War*. From the beginning we were hooked. My earliest memory of how FPL was taking over our lives was when my friend Andy, a staunch and passionate Liverpool fan, cheered a goal by Ruud Van Nistelrooy because he had him as captain. Andy celebrating a Manchester United goal was not just unheard of; it was absurd. I spent the first three years trying to win that mini-league and then, once I did, advanced onto improving my global rank.

My best-ever finish was 2,489th in the 2010/11 season. In addition, I have had one Top 25k finish, a Top 50k finish, two Top 100k finishes and five Top 250k finishes. My worst ever finish was 606k. My record is by no means poor but there are certainly many others out there who boast a better FPL history.

My strongest credentials for offering FPL advice do not come from my record, but from my 18 years of playing the game. In a game which is so governed by good fortune and strange anomalies, there is no substitute for experience. Some things may work brilliantly one season and be a terrible idea the next; that is the nature of the game. But over 18 years I have been able to spot trends and patterns which thread themselves between the chaos, to identify the things which may not work *all* the time but seem to work *most* of the time.

In September 2020, I suffered a sudden and strange medical issue which left me with partial hearing loss, fatigue and vestibular problems (my head got wobbly when I walked). As a result, I could not work or drive, amongst other things, for the best part of a year. When it became clear that this issue was going to be long term, I focused my energies on one of my biggest hobbies, writing. My starting point was writing about something which I was passionate about so I started jotting down my thoughts on FPL. Before I knew it, I had written everything I had learned in the 18 years I have been playing the game, and the first draft of this book was born.

A lot of the books, guides, strategies and other such information out there will give you detailed advice on how to follow the author's winning formula, but it is important to realise that the advice they offer is on *their* winning formula.

Write this down: <u>There is no universal winning formula.</u>

There are FPL managers out there who boast outrageously good FPL records, who rely heavily on statistics to make their FPL decisions. There are also those, with equally enviable records, who shun statistics and rely on gut feel, believing what they see with their eyes when they watch the matches. Both of these FPL managers are worth listening to, but they will offer you very different advice.

Also, having detailed football knowledge is not a requisite of being successful at FPL. I know many people who are excellent FPL managers but have a modest knowledge of football. Conversely, I have listened to podcasts featuring people whose comprehensive tactical knowledge of football blows me away, but they themselves have a mediocre FPL record. It could even be said that detailed knowledge of football can sometimes get in the way, forcing managers to overthink their decisions and overlook the simpler, more effective options.

Nor is past performance a reliable indicator of future success. At the time of writing the world #1, Ola Hovde, is on track to win the 2020/21 season. Prior to this season, he has never finished inside the top 1.5 million, despite playing for six seasons.

I have written this book having explored a multitude of different approaches over 18 seasons. Some approaches have worked once, but then not at all the next season. Others have been consistently bad and were therefore dropped, but there are aspects which I have found work consistently well, irrespective of whatever else I may be trying. Whenever I have abandoned these principles, my final overall rank has suffered.

This book contains 18 years' worth of trial and error.

HOW MUCH OF A FACTOR IS LUCK?

This is probably the toughest question to answer, and opinions on this vary. I wrote a blog post in January 2020 where I stated that success at FPL was:

"60% luck, 20% skill and 20% determination."

Having reflected on this further, I have since changed my mind. First, I would remove "determination" as a factor as this suggests you can win by sheer force of will, which of course you cannot. I would also redistribute the proportions between luck and skill so that luck was closer to 50%.

There is a massive temptation to look at FPL managers who consistently finish in the Top 10k and convince yourself that luck must be a minor factor but, on that point, I would say three things:

1) Those managers are very much in the minority. It may seem like there are lots of them, because their voices are so prominent in the FPL community, but that is because they are quickly identified by the largest FPL advice websites and snapped up to provide content for them. Their credentials are the currency by which we value their advice. It makes sense to listen to the guidance of these managers, but remember that they may have a playing style which differs from yours and, even if they don't, remember that most FPL managers, even the ones with the best records, frequently make decisions which do not work out.

2) A lot of those managers may still have their poor seasons ahead of them. I do not believe for a second

that an FPL manager who has six consecutive Top 10k finishes is going to play the game for another 20 years and not have a single season outside the Top 100k (or worse).

3) Have a think about what you are doing when you play FPL. You are essentially trying to predict the future.[2] If you believe that predicting the future accurately and consistently can be more skill than luck, then please help me with next week's lottery numbers.

I now believe that FPL success is:

- 50% luck
- 25% skill
- 25% self-discipline

Luck

I'm afraid neither I, nor anyone else, can help you with the most significant factor for success. Every week we place our faith in the FPL Gods, who can be very unkind. Recognising that luck is the biggest factor, and frequently reminding yourself of it, is an important step in your journey, particularly if you want to enjoy playing the game.

Skill

There are some people who are just downright good at FPL, either through innate ability or through finding the right blend of decision-making tools to guide their FPL transactions. There is a lot of very useful information out there (and I hope within

[2] What's more, you are trying to predict the future in a league which has garnered worldwide admiration for its unpredictable nature!

this book) and a multitude of different strategies you can adopt to your benefit which will give you a definite edge over most FPL managers.

Self-discipline

As for self-discipline, this is the factor over which we have the most control. That is not to say self-discipline is easy to master. FPL is a very emotional game. The highs can allow us to get carried away and the lows can make us want to give up. Only with self-discipline will you be able to stay grounded when things are going really well and pick yourself up off the floor when things are going horribly wrong. In either situation, it is important to stick to your principles.

***

What this balance of luck and ability (which, for the sake of argument, I will define as skill and self-discipline) means is that you will inevitably have some bad FPL managers who have really good records. Conversely, you will have really good FPL managers with poor records. For these managers, their luck (good or bad) is inversely proportional to their ability. That's just the way probability works. But *generally,* the highly skilled FPL managers will have better records and the bad FPL managers will have poorer records and this will become more aligned with time. The longer you play FPL, the more your ability is revealed, because luck is indiscriminately random, whereas ability is not.

I once heard a wonderful expression about FPL – I can't for the life of me remember who said it, but it really struck a chord with me. They said:

"Being good at FPL is all about putting yourself in the best position to be lucky."

That absolutely hits the nail on the head and should serve as encouragement for those who are new to the game and a reason to stay humble for those who consider themselves a veteran. Anyone can win FPL, even a first-timer. But it is *more likely* to be someone who is good at it.

I hope that once you have read this book you will feel better equipped to play FPL with focus, determination and patience. To exert control over the elements which you can influence. To drown out the noise and think clearly about your decisions and, above all else, to be able to enjoy the game.

PART 1:

PRE-SEASON

There is nothing quite like the feeling of joy in mid-to-late July when the overlords at FPL Towers open up their gates for squad registration and release all the player prices for the upcoming season. The barren, FPL-less months are finally over. It may yet be some time before the season officially kicks off, but the planning and the fun begins right now!

I think most enthusiasts will agree that there is nothing quite as pure as the blank canvas of those 15 greyed-out positions, itching to be filled with one of the countless combinations of players which will form your squad for Gameweek (GW) 1. Whatever happened last season is irrelevant. You may have finished in the Top 1k or had a season to forget but, at this moment, the slate is wiped clean.

Prior to the 2013/14 season, when the player prices were released, I created a simple spreadsheet, which I manually and painstakingly filled in. It set out the points each player had scored in the previous season and their cost in the new season. It had a separate column which recorded their points versus cost, to create a "points per £m" column. This was intended to capture a player's value so that I could identify the players who would give me the most "bang for my buck" across the different price points. That year I got off to a good start and finished the season in the Top 40k.

The season after, wanting more of the same, I blew the dust off the old spreadsheet and filled it in with the new data.[3] This time I created new columns. More data couldn't hurt, could it?

I recognised that players who had suffered long-term injuries were penalised by the old spreadsheet because their overall

[3] I am not going to lie; this ritual became one of the highlights of my year. Please don't judge me.

points were low, even if they had performed well when fit. This was an easy fix. I created a "points per minute" (PPM) column. I realised I could link this metric with my value ratio to create (forgive me) a "points per minute per £m" column. That year, I got off to a slow start, had too many squad issues and spent a large portion of the season fighting my way back up the ranks. I eventually finished in the Top 320k. A significant step back from the previous season and nowhere near the heights of the 2010/11 season.

I had fallen into the trap of focusing too much on one thing. In this case, numbers. I became too engrossed with things like value per minute and forgot to use common footballing sense. Some of those players with the highest PPM had such high values because they were not first choice, and the same was true in the follow-on season. Some of them were injury-prone and, inevitably, they got injured again the following season. I was distracted by statistics and neglected other important aspects of my initial squad, such as reliability, stability and consistency.

As I will discuss in this chapter, getting off to a good start is not an absolute requirement of having a good season but it makes life a hell of a lot easier. If you want to give yourself the best possible chance, there's a lot of work to do the moment the player prices are released. Time to roll up your sleeves and get stuck in.

GET A LOW ID

When you register for FPL, you are assigned a unique ID. You will find your ID by clicking on "View Gameweek history" under your team details. If you look at your URL, you will see a number (between /entry/ and /history). This is your unique ID.

The number you are assigned as your ID for the season is determined by how quickly you registered your team. If you were the first person in the world to register your team, then your ID would be 1. If you were the 599th, your ID would be 599 and so on.

With FPL league scoring, in the event of a tie-breaker, the team with the lowest number of transfers wins. If both managers made the same number of transfers, then the team with the lowest ID wins. This is incredibly unlikely to happen, but making the effort to register your team early could be worth it in the long run.

Also, having a low team ID makes it easier to remember should you ever need to use some of the great third-party apps or websites out there. As soon as I know FPL has opened for registration, I register and Auto-Pick a team, knowing I can tweak it later on. This gives me the best chance of obtaining a low ID.

POSITIONS

Goalkeepers (GK)

Goalkeepers, while incredibly important in real life, are bottom of the barrel when it comes to FPL. They are similar in price to defenders but without the chance of attacking returns.[4]

It can be tempting to pay extra for a premium GK because the logic follows that the better teams have a higher probability of keeping a clean sheet. The reality is that the lower-priced goalkeepers (for non-Top Six clubs) often outscore their more expensive counterparts. This is because goalkeepers from "lesser teams" often attract save and bonus points because, frankly, they have more work to do.

Some people like to have two playing GKs and rotate them between difficult fixtures. In my opinion, this takes up a larger than necessary chunk of budget (even if you go for two of the cheapest GKs) and gives you a constant selection headache throughout the season.

My preferred method of selecting a GK pairing is to find a keeper who you know is going to be first choice and is in the lowest price bracket (usually £4.5m); then, for your substitute keeper (who will probably never play) pick the second-choice keeper from the same team as your main GK (usually £4m). There you have it. A cheap and cheerful GK pairing which offers

---

[4] Although I distinctly remember Asmir Begovic scoring a remarkable goal for Stoke, against Southampton, in the 2013/14 season.

Edit: I have had to make this amendment just days before publication because Alisson Becker has scored a stunning 95th minute header in a must-win game against West Brom (so yes, it can happen!)

the added bonus that, in the event your main keeper gets injured, you do not need to rely on a precious transfer to sort the problem out. Your sub-keeper will automatically take over in subsequent Gameweeks.

Defenders (DEF)

When I first started playing FPL, selecting defenders was quite simple. Get the defenders that were in the lowest price bracket but who played for the best clubs. It didn't matter whether the defender was a centre back or full back, a clean sheet was a clean sheet and that's what defenders were for. In more recent times, using full backs as part of the attacking system is much more prevalent and this has created a little niche of points-returning juggernauts.

As is covered later, different seasons have their own unique pattern and so it is always worth avoiding stacking up on too many premium assets in any one position, and this is most true of defenders. These days, the best attack-minded defenders are priced around £6m to £7.5m, about the same price as a mid-range midfielder. This can be a bargain if the player is firing and a poor allocation of budget if not. I would recommend starting with at least one, maybe two premium defenders, but don't overspend your budget on your back line.

Certain fixtures which are in close geographical proximity are always deliberately rotated to avoid fan congestion in the area. For example, if Liverpool are playing at Anfield, Everton will play away that week. This is the same for any city which hosts two Premier League teams. This creates an interesting opportunity, whereby you can choose two defenders who will never both be playing away in the same Gameweek. Statistically a player is more likely to keep a clean sheet at home so, using this method, you can rotate the selected players each week so that the away defender is always on the bench and the home defender is in the starting XI.

I sometimes like to do this, but I won't allow it to impede a better combination of defenders. It is a "worth considering" rather than a "must do". Remember, a defender playing an easy team away may get a clean sheet over a defender playing tough opposition at home.

Midfielders (MID)

Midfield, in my eyes, is the most important position in FPL. Midfielders have two advantages over forwards, namely they get a point for a clean sheet, which forwards do not, and they get five points per goal, as opposed to four. In addition, they often play as part of a front three and, while not spearheading the attack, are expected to contribute as much, if not more, of the attacking returns as the traditional number 9.

Mo Salah, for example, is one of the greatest-ever FPL assets. He is arguably a forward, often playing in the number 9 role, but is classified as a midfielder by FPL. He is greedy, ruthless and gifted. He is everything you want in an FPL asset. As a midfielder he gets five points for a goal so we want to see him having a crack, not playing an unselfish pass across the box. Five points is better than three so, please Mo, keep being greedy.

In this sense, midfielders have the best of both worlds. How you stack up with midfielders really depends on the formation you want to play. A 3-4-3 is usually my default formation and hence I tend to opt for two premium midfielders, an upper-mid-priced one, a lower-mid-priced one and a budget midfielder for the bench.

I normally go for midfielders who play further forward, can play number 9 when needed, or are playmakers who occupy advanced positions and generate lots of assists. In the vast majority of cases, I would avoid having a holding or defensive midfielder in any price bracket. Defensive midfielders, in essence, are defenders who only get one point for a clean sheet. Their natural position on the pitch usually makes attacking returns scarce. Holding midfielders may dictate play and be required to make penetrating passes but, more often than not, they will get the "assist of the assist", which does not translate into points.

There are, of course, exceptions to this. In the 2020/21 season, Tomas Soucek scored an incredible number of goals from this position, mainly thanks to his aerial threat.

Forwards (FWD)

Your forward line is of paramount importance and it is crucial to get the right players, from an FPL perspective, in this position.

Take Roberto Firmino as an example. Firmino is a fantastic footballer and was a vital part of Klopp's title-winning Liverpool side. He is, however, to put it bluntly, a lousy FPL asset. His strength on the pitch is his team-oriented, selfless, hard-working mentality. He makes sacrificial runs constantly throughout every game. These runs drag defenders towards him, even though he has no intention of being passed to. This style of play creates gaps the other players can exploit. He deliberately takes himself out of the game, so that others have more space to score. This is an admirable and much-needed aspect of his game, but it is awful when viewed solely through the lens of points returns.

Of course, not all forwards are as selfless as Roberto Firmino. Some are downright goal-scoring assassins. Jamie Vardy. Harry Kane. Sergio Aguero. These are all explosive names, but they are expensive too.

Picking the right forwards is important, but not simple. For starters, you can only have three of them and they occupy a broad range of price points. I like to cover all bases so I will aim for one premium, one mid-range and one budget forward in my GW1 squad. As the campaign progresses, I usually end up with two budget forwards and one premium, but it is impossible to tell who these will be at the beginning.

Another thing to consider when bringing in a forward is what kind of frequency of returns you can expect. I call this the "consistent vs explosive" decision. Some forwards will deliver a steady trickle of points returns each week, nicking an assist here or there and generally providing you with something to smile about when the Gameweek is up. Raul Jimenez in the 2019/20 season is a good example of this.

Alternatively, you could go for an explosive forward. We are talking double-digit hauls, hat-tricks and FPL glory. Sergio Aguero always springs to mind when I think about explosive returns. The trouble with explosive forwards is quite often you will have to suffer periods of blanks before you get to the big, juicy returns. Over the course of a season a consistent returner of points and an explosive returner of points may offer you a similar total; the difference is how you come by the points. There is no greater feeling than a double-digit haul, especially if you captained the player, but the blanks are painful. The danger with explosive options is that you end up rotating between a number of explosive forwards and continually get nothing. Conversely, if you get the rotation right, it can make a positive difference to your rank.

I always got on very well with Sergio Aguero and I was saddened when he announced that he would be leaving Manchester City at the end of the 2020/21 season and subsequently had to retire from football for medical reasons. I generally managed to get him in at the right moments and not suffer too badly when I transferred him out. But I have always had a difficult relationship with Harry Kane. During a season, it often becomes clear that I need to bring in Kane and I always grimace when this happens because I can almost guarantee I will miss the boat with him.

The sweet spot is obviously to try and find a "consistently explosive" forward but, for some reason, this seems to be something of a rarity. If you are going to go explosive over consistent then make sure you have the patience to put up with the blanks.

Formations and bench

I've already covered my feelings on the goalkeeper position. Your sub-keeper will probably never be used, so use him as cheap cover for your main keeper which will mean you don't even have to think about a replacement.

I generally play a 3-4-3 or a 3-5-2 and so two of my three (non-GK) bench slots will be taken up by defenders. I will always try to go for two of the cheapest defenders who I know will play. My intention is that these defenders, for the most part, will stay on the bench, to be called upon only as needed. Sometimes, if one of my main three defenders has a particularly difficult fixture, I will rotate him for one on my bench with a stronger fixture.

When I play 3-4-3, my benched midfielder will generally be a cheap enabler.[5] Again, one who will play the full 90 minutes. Quite often value can be found in a holding midfielder (or defender) with a particular trait, such as aerial threat from set pieces. If the planets align then you may find that your budget enabler comes off the bench on the same Gameweek he scores a header.

Even when I am playing 3-5-2, my budget forward will always be one I feel I can rely on. I often see managers who find the cheapest possible player to fill this position (often a £4.5m enabler who isn't first choice). For me, this is a waste of a valuable position.

[5] The cheapest available players (£4m goalkeeper and defender, £4.5 midfielder and forward), who enable you to afford higher-value players elsewhere.

GENERAL PRINCIPLES

For the sake of your own sanity, you will want to kick off the season with some strong scores, and your initial squad is key to this. After 18 years of mixed starts, I have learned some general principles which can help get you off to a flying start.

Pre-season analysis

When setting out my initial squad, one of my primary objectives is to reduce the number of players who won't start to as small a number as possible. This involves being as sure as you can that the player you are selecting is going to be first choice. A good way of doing this is to follow pre-season friendlies closely.

Yes, some Premier League managers will use pre-season as an opportunity to fiddle and experiment with formations and systems, but largely (and particularly as the games get closer to the commencement of the season) they will start to reveal their preferred starting XI and how they plan to use their substitutions. Not only does this give you a better chance of selecting players who will start, but it increases the probability of being able to identify what I like to refer to as "The One".

Finding "The One"

I define "The One" as that player who outstrips all expectations and is priced very low. Effectively, this is a player you buy as a bench warmer and soon end up playing in your starting XI every week. The One is often a player who is played Out of Position (OOP) – that is to say, incorrectly categorised by FPL – but this is not always the case.

In the 2018/19 season it was Aaron Wan-Bissaka at Crystal Palace (correctly categorised as a defender), while in the 2019/20 season it was John Lundstram of Sheffield United. So successful was Lundstram's season, he earned the nickname "Lord Lundstram" and gained instant legendary status within the FPL community.

By tracking the pre-season statistics (and there are a number of great resources available which will do the hard data graft for you), it became abundantly clear that not only was Lundstram seemingly a first-choice player, but Chris Wilder was also playing him in midfield, despite FPL categorising him as a defender. I did not know this because I have an encyclopaedic knowledge of Championship teams, but because I did proper research during pre-season.

Although no one at the time could possibly have predicted just how solid the Sheffield United defence would turn out to be in the 2019/20 season, the prospect of a £4m midfielder who was nailed on to start, and who could pick up both clean sheets and six points per goal, was irresistible. Without pre-season analysis, I wouldn't even have known who John Lundstram was. As it was, I did my homework and had him in from the very beginning.

Spreading the risk

As the season progresses, you will get a feel for which teams are worth doubling, or even tripling, up on.[6] After Project Restart in the 2019/20 season, I tripled up on three Manchester United assets and they made a devastating trio. Often all three would get me returns in the same match, assisting each other

[6] You are allowed a maximum of three players from any one team. Doubling up is having two players from that team; tripling is having three players from that team.

and practically rolling around in the bonus points and throwing them in the air with glee.

At the beginning of a season, however, putting all your eggs in any one basket can be risky. The barren summer months can do strange things to teams. Whether it be new signings, tactical changes or perhaps just the lack of football abruptly halting a team's momentum, a team will often start out very differently to how they finished the previous campaign. If a team is going to flop at the beginning of a season, you don't want to own three of their players.

Instead, spread the risk across as many teams as you can. If a team is firing on all cylinders, then you can start to phase in more players from that team. If a team has got off to an awful start then you only have one player to shift out.

I am not saying you should aim to have 15 players from different teams, but try to limit the number of double-ups to a few and steer clear of triple-ups altogether until the season unfolds.

With all that said – and as we will discover later in the book – there are always exceptions to these general rules.

Before the 2021/22 season kicked off, Liverpool's Andy Robertson picked up an injury which was to see him sidelined for the opening matches of Liverpool's Premier League campaign. My thoughts went instantly to Kostas Tsimikas who, at the time, was the most likely alternative to fill in at left back. I checked out his price, which was £4m. This was an absolute gift. A £4m defender, for one of the best defences in the league, who just happened to be effectively drilled into playing in an advanced role. As I considered this move, it became apparent that the online FPL community was also mulling it over, with Tsimikas featuring in more and more drafts.

For me, there were two problems with bringing him in. One general, one personal. First, the danger was that any surplus cash generated by downgrading a premium defender to Tsimikas (for many this was Robertson himself) would be re-distributed amongst the squad and then, when Robertson came back from injury (which turned out to be earlier than expected – in GW3), the route back to "normality" would be difficult. The second problem, personal to me, is that I was acutely aware that this was the season after I had launched this book, in which I stated (as above) that managers should *"steer clear of triple-ups altogether"* in pre-season. As I already owned Salah and Alexander-Arnold, I couldn't bring in Tsimikas without going against my own advice, which, for obvious reasons, I didn't want to do.

I resisted bringing in Tsimikas until the very end, but it kept nagging at me. To bring the Greek full back in, Ben White (£4.5m) would have to make way and then Lewis Dunk (£5m) would be dropped to the bench. This would mean, aside from the aforementioned benefit, I would also strengthen my bench with a better option. Also, because I was switching one budget option for another, I wouldn't have surplus cash to squander and therefore box myself in when Robertson came back. As long as I switched Tsimikas to another budget defender, when the time came, I wasn't creating a problem for myself.

The only reason not to do it, therefore, was to avoid being contradictory. This started to feel like I was about to waste a golden opportunity for the wrong reasons. If I hadn't written this book, then there would be no issue after all.

In the end, I brought in Tsimikas just before the deadline. Ben White went the other way and Dunk dropped to the bench. In GWs 1–2, Tsimikas scored 17 points (White and Dunk got one and eight points respectively). When I heard that Robertson was back in contention earlier than expected, I shifted Tsimikas out for Tino Livramento[7] so that the value gained from the initial transfer could be captured while ensuring I had a regular starter providing bench cover.

I shudder to think that I almost didn't do this because I was worried about what I had committed to paper. As always, there are exceptions to a rule, and if FPL ever presents you with a gift (which it so rarely does) then think hard before turning it down.

Reliability

It may seem boring but there is great merit in selecting players (particularly your premium players) who have a proven pedigree in FPL. Players like Mo Salah, Kevin De Bruyne and Harry Kane have shown that they can be points magnets consistently over a number of seasons. You will find such players at various price points and in most positions. Their Total Points from previous seasons can be found in their Player Profile. Of course, any season could be *the* season a particular player stops returning points (as we saw with Kevin De Bruyne in the 2020/21 season and Harry Kane in the 2021/22 season) but, generally, you are in safer hands with a player with a consistent history.

Don't avoid players because they play for rival teams

Many managers avoid players because they play for a rival team and they can't quite bring themselves to own players from a team they loathe.

[7] Which later proved to be a very good decision indeed.

Imagine this. You're an avid Everton fan at the beginning of the 2021/22 season. You are planning to go the entire campaign without owning Salah or Alexander-Arnold. I might not go as far as to say that this is FPL suicide, but it is putting yourself at a severe disadvantage.

It may be that your feelings on the matter are so strong that owning these players will literally ruin the enjoyment of your FPL season. If this is the case, then don't bring them in. As we will discover later in the book, enjoying FPL should be your #1 priority. But you should do it knowing full well that avoiding rival players is (likely to be) sub-optimal.

Set-piece takers

Find out who takes the set pieces for each team and factor this into your decision-making process. If a team has a guaranteed primary penalty taker, then this player will earn points, even if a different player did all the hard work to be awarded the penalty. Likewise, free kick and corner takers will have an increased chance of goal involvement. If it is a toss-up between two players, then why not go for the one who takes the set pieces?

Managers will often use the summer break to change their set-piece takers so, if you are bringing in a player because they were on penalties last season, do some research to ensure that this is still the case. This is another good reason to do your homework in pre-season.

Avoid disgruntled players

As those who selected Harry Kane at the beginning of the 2021/22 season will fully understand, selecting a player who is disgruntled with their club prior to the season starting can be an expensive risk to take.

Kane's publicly expressed desire to leave Spurs, his disappointment when he was not released to join Manchester City, and his subsequent decision to extend his family holiday – meaning he re-joined his training duties late – was well documented and there for all to see. Despite this, a surprising number of FPL managers (just shy of a million) still included him in their GW1 squad. He went on to blank in 12 out of his first 13 fixtures.

In the challenging and demanding Premier League, players must be at the peak of their physical and mental prowess to succeed. FPL managers should be wary of any disgruntled players until evidence of good form dispels that caution.

Common traps to avoid

1. Seeking instant gratification

It is, of course, possible to be *too* eager for a good start. With limited free transfers (covered later), your initial squad will form the backbone of your FPL campaign. It is important to appreciate that you and your squad are in it for the long haul. I have seen many managers make short-term decisions for short-term gains and then spend the next six Gameweeks falling behind, because what looked like a great squad for GW1 was actually an awful squad for the five subsequent Gameweeks.

2. Looking *too* far ahead

As with most things, it is also possible to go too far the other way. Don't get overly concerned with a bad clump of fixtures which start around GW6; there will be plenty of time to tweak your squad gently between now and then so that you avoid the bad patch. Likewise, I wouldn't advocate having a player in your initial squad who is injured, or liable to be rotated, just because at some point they will be better.

Strike a balance between points 1 and 2 and set up your initial squad with the first six to eight Gameweeks in mind.

3. Taking chances on unproven players

There are usually a couple of new and exciting summer signings who are high-profile players from elsewhere in the world who have never played in the Premier League. The quality of the Premier League should not be underestimated. It stands apart from any other league in the world. The competition is fierce. If a team in the relegation zone beats a team in the Top Four, it is certainly surprising, but it is not unheard of in the way it is in other leagues. Naturally, players joining the Premier League can take time to adapt in their maiden season.

Compare Timo Werner and Jamie Vardy at the beginning of the 2020/21 season. Werner (an exciting new prospect from the Bundesliga) was £9.5m and Vardy (the previous year's Premier League Golden Boot winner and consistent returner of points in FPL) was £10m. Vardy, despite his proven pedigree, was owned by just over a million managers. Werner, who had had a great season for RB Leipzig but had never played in the Premier League, was owned by over 2.8 million managers. In their first six appearances Werner scored 29 points (average of 4.8 points per game) compared to Vardy's 55 points (9.2 points per game).

When Timo Werner first joined the Premier League, he was interviewed and asked how he was adapting to the Premier League. He commented after Chelsea's opening game against Brighton that he had never played against such big defenders before:

> *"Yeah, Premier League is different football because I think defenders... I have never played against three defenders like this so tall, so big massive defenders."*

The week after he made this comment, he was due to face Virgil van Dijk.

Some players adapt incredibly quickly to the Premier League – names such as Luis Suarez and Bruno Fernandes spring to mind – but, for most, there is a period of bedding in when they are not at their best. Don't forget that, for a non-UK player, it is not just the Premier League they are having to adapt to, but a totally new lifestyle. Quite often these players are moving country, finding new schools for their children, having to learn a new language and find a new home. These are all significant life events and while these players will have the support and finances to make the transition easier, it will still take its toll on a person.

The first six Gameweeks are where, as managers, we will face the most problems, find out how a season is likely to play out, and take note of which players are firing and which players are flopping. Why then, during this already volatile period would you want to add an unknown factor into the mix, namely: will this player adjust to the Premier League instantly or not?

It is always nice to be first to a bandwagon and get points which others have missed out on but I think it is much better to allow others to pioneer the risky routes first. At the beginning, stick to solid, reliable and proven options. As the season progresses, observe other managers and judge their success before jumping on a new craze. You may miss out on a couple of Gameweeks of points but you may also dodge a bullet.

The same can also be said for world-class players who have been away from the Premier League for a while and are making a return.

Early in the 2021/22 season, Premier League fans from all over the world (and particularly those from the red half of Manchester) were thrilled by the shock signing of Cristiano Ronaldo from Juventus. The ramifications of this signing sent shockwaves through the FPL community. Managers, who were still getting to grips with the new season, suddenly found themselves with a significant decision to make. Do you dare to go without (arguably) the greatest player in the world? Or do you put your transfer plans in the bin to bring him in for GW4? This decision was further complicated by the fact that many managers were also scrabbling to bring in Romelu Lukaku who, after a phenomenal season with Inter Milan, was now the new Chelsea front man and, many argued, the missing piece in an otherwise perfect jigsaw.

For various reasons, I decided to stick with my team and opt for neither, electing instead to target Lukaku when Chelsea's fixtures turned in GW7.[8] My main reason for not going with Ronaldo was that I wasn't convinced Manchester United were set up to accommodate the "new" Cristiano Ronaldo. Juventus built their team around Ronaldo and relied heavily on feeding the Portuguese legend with service from the wings. Indeed, the stats showed that Juventus topped the tables for deliveries from crosses of all Serie A teams.

Manchester United, however, were not set up this way. Much of United's attacking threat came from the likes of Marcus Rashford, who prefers to cut inside and shoot rather than cross.

---

[8] This turned out to be an ill-fated decision as he picked up a significant injury in GW8 which saw him sidelined for months.

Aaron Wan-Bissaka (to put it politely) is not renowned for his crossing ability. The inclusion of Ronaldo would inevitably dampen Bruno Fernandes' goal potential, which seemed counter-intuitive given how prolific he had been in the previous season. While I could understand why United fans were excited, I wanted to see just how tactically adaptable Ole Gunnar Solskjaer was before ripping my team apart to fit Ronaldo in.

My reluctance to bring in Ronaldo was almost instantly punished when he scored a brace in his debut game against struggling Newcastle United. He also bagged a goal in the next Gameweek when they faced West Ham. After that my prediction came true. Manchester United looked awkward and sluggish; a team without a plan. This led to a string of awful performances and, ultimately, cost the manager his job.

Ronaldo went on to blank in 14 out of his next 19 matches. A poor rate of returns for a £12.5m forward. Likewise Lukaku, who admittedly had less time to prove himself, only returned in two out of his seven appearances.

Even world-class players, with proven pedigree in the Premier League, can find themselves struggling when suddenly dropped into a team which has since moved on.

Take note of your first proper draft

Once my team is registered and the squad auto-picked (to get a low ID), I set aside some quiet time when I can properly focus on my squad, knowing I won't be interrupted. This time is spent removing all the auto-picked players and replacing them with the ones I want.

At this stage, I am doing it "freestyle" – not really looking at fixtures or stats but instead trying to shape the team using my instincts. I will have spent all summer thinking about which players I want for the season ahead. Now it's time to see if I can fit them all in. This first draft is not constrained by detail. It is bigger-picture thinking; it is my "gut feel" speaking.

Now, as we know, the final draft will look very different from this initial draft. We can't ignore fixtures and it may happen that the midfielder who you've had down as a "lock" in your mind actually plays for a team which starts the season on a really difficult run of games, and perhaps it would be best to bring him in when the fixtures are somewhat kinder. Also, the transfer window will still be open, meaning players will come and go. Players may get injured in pre-season or fall out of favour with their team's new manager. All these things will have an impact on your decisions – and so they should. But I advise everyone to do two things:

First, put the stats and fixtures away when you initially have a play with your squad and let your intuition guide you to create your first proper draft. Second, take a note/screenshot/sketch of it before it gets lost in the torrent of changes to come.

It has been scientifically proven that instinct is the result of highly complex and unconscious analysis of large amounts of information. We might think we are clever, delving into stats and analysing fixture difficulty, but the forces which inform our latent intuition are a lot smarter, and they are certainly worth listening to.

If you get towards the GW1 deadline, have tweaked your team to oblivion and feel unsettled and unsure about it – and this sometimes happens – then go back to your first proper draft and get some inspiration from it.

RULE CHANGES

At the time of writing, the structure and rules of FPL have been remarkably consistent for some time, but it is important to note that the game has evolved greatly from when I first started playing in 2004. Back then, you couldn't roll a transfer, chips were things you ate, and you got one Wildcard each season. Once it was gone, it was gone.

FPL don't tend to make a great big song and dance when they change something, so make sure you check the Rules and FAQs in the Help section before you start each season. Even a slight change to the scoring system could influence your strategy, so make sure the first thing you do is get yourself up to date and check there are no changes. If you are a member of the FPL community and there are new rules (or, dare I say it, chips) introduced to the game then you will not be able to escape detailed and frantic discussion about it.

KEEP UP TO DATE

There will invariably be ten-trillion versions of your GW1 squad as you tweak, refine, nudge, alternate, disregard, evaluate and reconsider your options. This is all part of the fun and magic of FPL. For me, it is the very best part.

As fun as it is, it *will* get tiring, and the closer you get to the season starting, the more riddled with self-doubt you will become. Eventually you will reach a point where you just want to stop making changes to your squad and settle down on what will be the final version.

When you reach this point, make sure you keep your eye on the news for any injuries or new signings which could threaten the chances of one (or more) of your players starting. Don't get too concerned with a small injury doubt. If your team is as good as it is going to be and you are finally happy with it, don't wreck it by transferring out a key player because of a 25% chance of him not playing. That is what your bench is for. If, however, the injury seems a little longer term, you may have to make changes to your squad at the last minute and find yourself thrust into the whole process again.

GOLDEN RULE #1:

Set up your GW1 squad to cover all price points, in each position, and leave at least £0.5m in the bank.

As discussed, a good start in FPL is key to a good finish and a good GW1 squad is key to a good start. The beginning of the season, however, is one of the most turbulent periods and there are few FPL managers, even amongst the most successful, who do not spend the first quarter of the season putting out fires and adapting to unexpected changes.

No matter how much research you do, how much sense your squad makes on the basis of last season's performances, or what you have witnessed in pre-season, you cannot get inside the heads of the real-life Premier League managers. In addition, the summer break can disrupt a good run of form.

In the 2019/20 season a great many managers set up their initial squad to contain at least two, and often three, Bournemouth players and with good reason. During the 2018/19 season, Bournemouth's attacking prowess was surprisingly good. Even in defeat, Bournemouth would scrap away to get goals. The trio of King, Wilson and Fraser offered tremendous value. In the subsequent season, Bournemouth couldn't get out of the starting blocks and were eventually relegated to the Championship.

In life, the best predictor of future performance is past performance, and so it is with FPL. That does not always mean that history will repeat itself. FPL managers are often taken by surprise as to how a season begins. Sometimes a team which you had written off performs well from the very beginning and vice versa. Sometimes this trend drops off at some point and reality sets in, but sometimes it continues to surprise you right until the end of the season – like Leicester City in 2015/16.

The point is that these significant swings cannot be accurately predicted by anyone, so we must ensure we are in a position to capitalise on them when they become apparent. The first part of this is having a good spread of price points across all the positions. There are a number of different ways to achieve this, and many different templates available to facilitate different types of set-up, but how I like to tackle it is simple.

Set up a spreadsheet, even before the player prices are released, and rather than populate it with names of players you think you will want, fill it with £s.

You know your budget is going to be £100m, so spread that out amongst your entire squad. It's harder to do than you think. Don't stop until you've got at least one premium, one mid-range and one budget price point occupying each position (for this exercise, I class GK and DEF as one position). Keep your bench cheap and cheerful (but not filled with £4m fodder who stand no chance of playing). Make sure, when you are finished, that you have £0.5m in the bank. What you now have is a pricing template to help guide your player choices.

When registration opens, simply pick players to fit the price points you have set in your template and mould your team around it. Don't worry too much about the odd £1m discrepancy here or there. If your template says that you can have a £9m forward and a £12m forward, then don't worry if the combination you want actually costs £8m and £11m. This is a guide, not a tablet of stone.

The point to all this is to set up a squad which is dynamic and flexible. When the season kicks off, and all the cards are thrown up into the air, it can take three to four Gameweeks before you start to get a real feel for what is an anomaly and what is a definite trend in the new season. Being able to quickly adapt to this is vital to steering your squad onto the winning course early.

You never know which position, or indeed which price point, the big-hitting or value generating players are going to come from so it makes sense to have all bases covered so that you can transfer any of them in at the drop of a hat.

Imagine an FPL manager who has invested heavily in five midfielders and paid for it by having a front three of budget forwards. Their midfield might well be the envy of the FPL community, but what happens when it becomes abundantly clear that Player A, a forward priced at an eye-watering £11m, is going to be the next "must have" player? The manager who has over-invested in midfield is going to be looking at two, and most likely more, transfers to get him in. During that time, they are going to have to make some tough decisions regarding the starting XI in order to make room for Player A. Whereas the manager who picked Player B (£12m) to occupy that space can react immediately.

As for the £0.5m, this is a little trick I picked up to beat price changes. Previously, I always felt I had to maximise my squad potential by investing every last drop of cash from the budget across the 15 slots. I mean, why would anyone waste money? Here's why:

I have repeatedly highlighted that the beginning of any season is one of the most volatile periods, and the same is true for player price changes. As FPL managers run around like headless chickens trying to correct all their squad issues, they do so with a very limited data set. Over the course of a season a large number of viable transfer options present themselves; however, early on in the season this is usually narrowed down to a few clear choices and everyone flocks to bring these players in. This causes sharp price changes as managers offload their blanking assets to bring those top scorers in. In addition, all players are initially priced as a multiple of £0.5m. You never get any players who are initially priced as £10.3m – this happens over time with £0.1m increments. What this effectively means, to someone who has spent all their budget, is that a £0.1m price change is the practical equivalent of a £0.5m price change.

If you are blown away by Player X (£9m – you don't own), who scored a brace at the weekend, and are underwhelmed by Player Z (£9m – you do own), who blanked, then you may well want to make the switch. The problem is, others will have spotted Player X too and, if enough people transfer him in, his price will go up by £0.1m very quickly. Straight away you are in trouble because you have no money in the bank. Now you have to make other changes, which are potentially sub-optimal, in order to bring in Player X. In addition, the chances are you are going to have to take a points hit to do this, or do it over two Gameweeks in which you must continue to be a non-owner of the asset you have targeted.[9] Now, replay this scenario if you had kept £0.5m in the bank.

The combination of having a good distribution of price points across your entire squad and a sneaky half a million in your back pocket served me well in the 2020/21 season, and I really wish I had been doing this for much longer. It's also good from a psychological point of view, being able to jump on a bandwagon without having to rip your team apart in the early stages of the season.

---

[9] A points hit is taken when a transfer is made once the Free Transfer has been used (see Glossary, "Hits").

***

If you are anything like me, you will be pretty exhausted by now and will be practically begging for the season to start just so you can have a rest from the endless variations of player combinations which have been haunting your dreams for the last few weeks. But you know as well as I do that the emotional rollercoaster is just about to begin. Strap yourselves in because the season is upon us.

PART 2:
THE GAMEWEEKS

In the 2019/20 season, I got off to a shocking start. Nothing I did went right. I don't recall having too many squad issues at the beginning, so I can't really blame the poor start on injury or rotation. It was just one of those frustrating times when all my transfers were poorly timed.

You may remember the phenomenon that was Teemu Pukki, who had an incredible start for Norwich that year. He was in the main draft of my initial GW1 squad for most of pre-season before a last-minute raft of changes led to him making way for Shane Long.[10] Pukki absolutely smashed it in those opening Gameweeks but eventually faded out into nothingness when Norwich entered the harder times which newly promoted teams often suffer. I transferred Pukki in and out on two occasions. He blanked in every Gameweek in which I owned him and returned in the rest. The chances must have been astronomically low of getting it as wrong as I did. This was one of many such issues.

By GW5, I was ranked 3.76m. This prompted me to take action, and I played my Wildcard in GW6. With six weeks' worth of data, I had a decent feel for how the season was playing out. I knew which players to target, and which to avoid. What followed was eleven straight green arrows which saw my rank jump as high as 191k in GW17. I was in heaven and couldn't believe I was on target for a Top 100k finish, particularly after such a horrendous start.

What happened thereafter was a bit of a mystery and, if I had to put my finger on it, I would say I clung too tightly to the post-Wildcard squad that had served me so well. I failed to adapt to the subtle movements which were occurring in the league and therefore my rank rises stagnated.

---

[10] Yes, you heard me right, Shane Long.

The Disaster of Double Gameweek 24 (as mentioned in the Introduction) compounded matters and, by GW29, my overall rank had dropped to 902k.

GW30 never happened because of Covid-19 until it was eventually replaced by GW30+ when Project Restart kicked off. The new, Covid-secure footballing schedule was kind to me and, by the penultimate Gameweek, I had clawed back 600k places with a rank of 302k.

An idiotic transfer and uncharacteristically random captaincy decision in the final Gameweek massively backfired, and I dropped 125k places, finishing up with a final overall rank of 427k. My second worst in 18 years.

***

The purpose of this tour of my 2019/20 campaign is to illustrate the huge swings which can happen during a season. From this brief glimpse, I want you to take away two things:

Firstly, a bad start is not the end of the world. Even if your rank is very poor (borderline shameful), you can turn things around in a relatively short space of time. Never lose hope.

Secondly, just because you have enjoyed a great start and have a sky-high overall rank, do not get too contented. The FPL Gods can chew you up and spit you out in just a few weeks.

It can be a very cruel game and, whatever your playing style, it is important to be self-disciplined through the entire campaign, right up to the very last Gameweek.

WHAT DO YOU WANT TO ACHIEVE?

An important question to ask yourself when playing FPL is "what am I trying to achieve?" This might seem silly. We are all aiming to get as many points as we physically can in a season, of course.

Aiming for the #1 global spot is an admirable goal and, although you or I are unlikely to ever achieve it, getting as close to it as possible is a logical objective to pursue. The reality is that your strategic approach to the game should be adaptable based on what it is you are trying to achieve.

There may be a rival in the office who has beaten you two seasons in a row despite clearly knowing less than you do about football. It may be that you are such a consistent high achiever that you always come #1 in all of your mini-leagues and have set your sights on your first Top 100k (or Top 10k or Top 1k) overall finish.

Once you have your objective clearly defined, you can stop at any given point in the season and see where you are relative to it. This should have a bearing on the decisions you make. This is where FPL strategy gets a little bit more advanced, so bear with me.

Player ownership

In simple terms players are either highly owned or owned by few managers (the latter are known as differentials). Of course, there is a middle band of players that you wouldn't consider being highly owned or differentials. However, for the purposes of this exercise, let us split them neatly into two categories.

We now need to view these categories from two different perspectives. Players we own and players we don't. This gives you:

- Highly owned players you don't own
- Highly owned players you do own
- Differentials you don't own
- Differentials you do own

Imagine four players (one from each category) and, for illustration, let us say all four players return a favourable number of points in the next Gameweek. Let's consider the impact these players will have on your overall rank:

- Highly owned player you don't own – this player will be **highly damaging** to your overall rank (many managers own him, yet you do not)
- Highly owned player you do own – this player will have a **positive but minimal** impact on your overall rank (you will benefit from him doing well, but so will many others)
- Differential you don't own – this player will have a **negative but minimal** impact on your overall rank (you will not benefit from his points return, but neither will many others)
- Differential you do own – this player will have a **strong positive** impact on your overall rank (you benefit from him doing well but few others will share that benefit)

Remember that compound ownership can create a differential. You may own a combination of highly owned players who form a differential because that mixture doesn't occur very often.

To complicate matters further you have Effective Ownership (EO). This is the percentage of managers who own a player, accounting for those who have captained that player (effectively multiplying ownership by two – or by three if the Triple Captain chip has been played) and those who have benched that player (effectively removing them from the ownership calculation). If a player's EO is higher than 100% then this can be problematic. If you have captained this player and he hauls – i.e. brings in more than one return in a game – you could find that it has a very minor impact on your rank. Even worse, if you have not captained this player then you could find that his haul damages your rank despite you owning him.

In GW32 of the 2020/21 season, I gave Harry Kane the armband. Tottenham were the only team with a double Gameweek and had two relatively easy fixtures, so this was a straightforward decision. This Gameweek was the perfect opportunity to play the Triple Captain chip (unfortunately I had already played mine). As a result, so many people played the Triple Captain chip on Kane, that his Effective Ownership in my rank tier was 215%. This meant that despite Kane being my captain, I *lost* rank when he returned.

Sword vs shield

If you are happy with your overall rank and do not want it to drop, then you can shape your team to be full of highly owned players – this is also known as a "template team" (you will often hear people in the FPL community discussing how template, or not, a team is). The quintessential template team is the one which comprises the most highly owned players, without being unobtainable because of budgetary or formation restrictions.

If your highly owned team does well, then you will do well, but so will many others. Your rank will increase, but not by much. Conversely, if your highly owned team does poorly, then your rank will drop, but not by much (because many others will also suffer). Therefore, your highly owned players are your "shield". Having many highly owned players protects your rank.

If you are not happy with your rank and wish it to be higher, then you will need to invest in differentials. If your team of differentials does well, then your rank will skyrocket. These players who have brought you so many points are owned by so few others that, while most squads are suffering, yours has done well. Unfortunately, the converse is also true, and this is one of the difficult aspects of chasing rank.

If your team of differentials does badly, your rank will suffer enormously. Not only have you had a low-scoring Gameweek, but many others have done better. Therefore, your differentials are your "sword". As with many actual swords, differentials are double-edged. Owning differentials can help you cut your way through the ranks, but they can also make you fall even deeper into the chasms of obscurity.

To bring this back to what you want to achieve, you need to look closely at what is going on around your particular rank tier. The template team amongst managers in the Top 10k is likely to look very different to the overall template team. There are many different tools out there which can help you assess ownership of the various rank tiers. The website www.livefpl.net is a tremendous (and completely free to use) resource created by Ragabolly. He has spent years working on the code to make the website do what it does today. Using this you can, amongst many other things, assess average player ownership in each of the rank tiers. If you are aiming for a Top 10k finish, and are currently in the Top 100k tier, then you can use this ownership information to decide how to apply the shield, and how to apply the sword.

A word of caution: it is easy to fall into an overly statistical rabbit hole trying to chase rank. By all means use these tools, but not at the expense of the other aspects covered in this book. I firmly believe that you should make the right decision irrespective of a player's EO. If having concluded your research there is a standout decision, then go for that player whether he is highly owned or not. If it is close between two (or more) players, then you can use EO statistics to guide you to a decision based on whether you would like to gain or protect rank.

You may be reading this thinking, *"I don't care about rank, I just want to beat Derek from Accounting."* Well, the same logic applies; it is just much easier to implement. If you are behind Derek from Accounting in your work mini-league (and you both have similar teams) then you will need to take a punt on players he doesn't have to try and get one over on him. If you are ahead of Derek from Accounting, and wish to stay ahead, you may want to consider matching his premium assets so that, if he gets a haul from that player, so do you. That way, he is forced to take more risks than you to catch up.

There is another element to all this which is well worth pointing out. Differentials are differentials for a reason. Players tend to be highly owned at the beginning of a season either because they are a new and exciting prospect or they did well in the previous season. During the campaign, a player's ownership tends to rise because they have been performing well. At the opposite end of the spectrum, a player's ownership either falls, or stays low, due to poor performance. By targeting differentials, you are deliberately bringing in players *who the majority of managers do not think are going to return points.* This is not necessarily a reason to avoid doing it, but you should take on differential players with your eyes wide open.

Does prioritising mini-leagues affect overall rank?

This was a question I asked myself at the beginning of the 2021/22 season. I have always been curious as to why I suffered a string of poor finishes after a relatively good period in my FPL career. After all, one should *improve* with experience, not go backwards. Of course, with luck being such a prominent factor in FPL, there was always the chance that I just had a few unlucky seasons. However, I couldn't rid myself of this nagging suspicion that there was more to it.

I then decided to do some digging in my FPL history and uncovered something interesting.

As mentioned earlier, I spent my first three seasons trying to win *Hogs of War*, the only mini-league I was in at the time. After winning that, my focus switched to improving my overall rank, which was my priority for many years. Then, at the beginning of the 2014/15 season, I took part in a cash league, which became my focus for several years. In the 2020/21 season I stopped participating in the cash league and went back to focusing on my overall efforts.

When analysing my past seasons, I realised I could divide my playing history into two parts: those Gameweeks where winning a mini-league was my primary objective and those where overall rank was my main objective.

The results of the analysis showed that my average OR over the 15 recorded seasons was 224k.[11] For those seasons in which I was actively participating in a mini-league rivalry – eight out of fifteen – my average OR was 297k. For those seasons in which I was not engaged in a mini-league rivalry (that is to say, it wasn't a priority) my average OR was 140k.

Obviously, there are other factors to consider when evaluating these results. However, it is difficult not to conclude that focusing on mini-league rivalries – or participating in cash leagues – has had an adverse effect on my overall rank.

The above highlights the importance of setting goals and objectives for the season ahead. It may be that participating in your friends' mini-league – or your work's cash league – is the focus you *want* to have because that's how you enjoy playing the game – and there is nothing wrong with this. But it is worth noting that if overall rank is important to you, then you may need to make sub-optimal decisions in one of your mini-leagues to do the best thing for your team from a global perspective.

For what it's worth, I have found that focusing on overall rank usually leads to success in your mini-leagues as well, although the converse is not true.

[11] I registered for the 2004/05 and 2005/06 seasons under a separate email address – since lost – and hence the data for these seasons is not available. This is why I only have data for 15 out of the 17 full seasons I have played FPL.

TRANSFERS

If you think about how FPL works, you don't actually have many things you can control, once you have set your initial squad. If you put your chips to one side (given that they only affect 5 out of 38 Gameweeks), then what is left that you can actually influence? Just three things. You can:

1. Set a captain
2. Decide who features in the starting XI
3. Transfer one player per Gameweek[12]

Captaincy is clearly important but, generally, there are a limited number of candidates you will select from your squad. Picking who goes on your bench is usually not too much trouble[13] and, for many managers, they will have filled their bench with cheap enablers, who may not even be first choice anyway. Even here your bench choices are limited by the number of valid formations available.

Making transfers, therefore, is the primary control you possess to influence your team's success. It is the navigation tool you use to steer your team through the entire campaign. The importance of transfer-making cannot be understated. What's more, the number of options is overwhelmingly large, and you have to narrow these down to just one change per week.

It is difficult to give generic advice on making transfers because the moves an individual makes will depend on that individual's

[12] Obviously more if you have rolled a free transfer or take a points hit.

[13] Although there are odd times when it is complete hell!

playing style and where a manager's team is, relative to their objectives, at any stage of the season. There are, however, a few general principles I use to govern my transfer decisions.

Upcoming fixtures

When you are making your transfer decisions, do not just think solely about the next Gameweek. If a transfer candidate has a mouth-watering fixture in the next Gameweek but then faces three of the Top Six teams in the following four games, then you are signing yourself up for a future headache.

It is, of course, possible to think too far ahead and get your knickers in a twist over fixtures which are so far down the line that even Nostradamus isn't worried. My sweet spot of fixture planning is usually between four to six Gameweeks. Use the Premier League website's FDR (Fixture Difficulty Rating), or one of the more complex "fixture tickers" available to paying members of Fantasy Football Hub or Fantasy Football Scout.[14] These tools will clearly show who has a good run of fixtures and who is going to struggle.

Please note that FDRs and fixture tickers are usually populated with pre-defined parameters of difficulty. That is to say, they don't consider changes that are apparent within the season. A newly promoted team may be given a rating of just 2 (easy) at the beginning but, over the course of the season, become a formidable opponent. The fixture rating for a team playing this opponent will continue to be 2 even though, in reality, it has become a much more difficult fixture. Use your common sense

[14] I currently use the FPL Fixture Difficulty Planner which can be found at www.footballfallout.com – this one is completely free and automatically organises fixtures by their difficulty (easiest to hardest) for a period of Gameweeks which you can alter to your preference.

and adjust these ratings in your own mind. Alternatively, there are several form-based fixture tickers out there which adjust the FDR on a week-by-week basis and therefore stay more relevant.

The "planned transfers" debate

There are differences of opinion when it comes to the "planned transfers" debate, also known as "booking in future transfers". Those in favour believe in having a mapped-out route of transfers to navigate through the Gameweeks, knowing which players they will transfer in several weeks in advance, like in a game of chess. Those who are against this method believe that it is a waste of time targeting players, Gameweeks in advance, because of the changing nature of FPL. After all, a single injury could scupper those plans.

As with most worthwhile debates, the answer lies somewhere in the middle. I frequently map out the next four to six Gameweeks and try to narrow down my transfer targets to a select few candidates. But I do this knowing that the plan is highly likely to change. New in-form players will emerge, teams who were once dominant will stop clicking, cheap £4m defenders who are starting regularly will start vying for our attention. This does not mean having a plan is a waste of time. Far from it. View your plan as a backbone of logic threading its way through the immediate future. As new information presents itself, you can evaluate your plan to see if it still works and, if it does not, make the required adjustments to bring it back on track or take advantage of better opportunities.

The British economist John Maynard Keynes famously said: *"When the facts change, I change my mind."* By all means have a plan. Just be prepared and willing to adapt it.

Form vs fixtures

This is the age-old debate, which has raged since before I played FPL and will continue to go on as long as the game exists. When it comes down to it, would you go for the player who is in good form or the player with the better fixture? I think, in general, this is a bit of a pointless question because both have their merits, and *both* are usually possible to find.

Instead, I look at it this way: which players have both form *and* fixtures on their side? More often than not, there is at least one candidate who this applies to, so why pick one or the other? If you were to put a gun to my head and make me choose, I would probably err (just) on the side of fixtures. Although, if you will allow me to elaborate on that before you pull the trigger, I would actually say that I am *less* inclined to care about fixtures for my premium players and *more* inclined to care about fixtures for my budget players.

When you have a Mo Salah or Kevin De Bruyne firing on all cylinders, it doesn't really matter who they are against; there's a good chance they're going to return. Conversely, if a budget striker is playing the worst defence in the league, again there's a good chance at getting a return there.

If you find yourself staring at a number of good options, analyse both form <u>and</u> fixtures. If a candidate ticks both boxes, then he has to be considered above a player who has only one or the other. Another way to look at the form vs fixtures dilemma in terms of transfer policy is like this:

- BUY players who have both form and fixtures on their side

- SELL players who have neither form nor fixtures on their side
- KEEP players who have one of the two

Put out fires first

If you are fortunate enough to find yourself in a position where all of your players, including your bench, are first choice, not injured or suspended and are not facing the chop because of some imminent new signing, then now is the time to start planning for the immediate future and fine tuning your squad.

Chances are at least one of your players is playing difficult opposition, and you can be certain that there are many players who you don't own who have both form and fixtures on their side. This is where you can start to make the difference to your points totals, one transfer at a time.

If, however, you have two players with long-term injuries, a player who only starts 50% of games, and a £4.5m third striker who doesn't even get brought on as a sub, then you need to put these fires out immediately. It does not matter how much another transfer makes sense or how worried you are that others are going to cash in on a haul which you will miss out on. You have some very basic housekeeping to attend to first. It may not be glamorous and it may not be exciting, but you will sorely regret not getting your squad back into shape.

There are unexpected benefits from solving minor squad issues ahead of making sexy, big-hitting transfers. The first of these is that swapping a playing premium asset for another playing premium asset is, often, the wrong thing to do, even if everything is pointing towards it being the right move. By putting out fires first, you can often avoid making a mistake.

Have a think about the weekly FPL Scout Selection. This is essentially like being able to play your Wildcard every week but, how often does it come near to the actual Kings of the Week (highest-scoring) team?[15] Practically never. The Kings of the Week teams are usually composed of a group of players you would not stop laughing at if someone had suggested them beforehand. By not being able to change your team as much as you would like, you will find that you "accidentally" capture some of these points hauls, even if they come from unlikely places.

Second, and important from a psychological perspective, a transfer which heals damage in your squad *feels* positive even if it doesn't yield results. The outgoing (injured) player is definitely going to get zero points. The one coming in may blank and get you just two points, but your net position is better in the immediate Gameweek and it has strengthened your squad for future Gameweeks.

On the other hand, a speculative transfer ("I think this player which I don't own will outscore this player which I do own") *only* feels positive if it is successful. If your outgoing player scores more than the one you brought in, you end up kicking yourself hard. *"Why the hell didn't I leave things alone?"* is an all-too-common outcry of an FPL manager. To make matters worse, you are also haemorrhaging points through the injured players you have neglected to sort out.

Team value

This is something I see a lot of managers getting overly concerned about, and I can't really understand why. If you build

[15] Both the Scout Selection and Kings of the Week can be found on the Official FPL website each week.

up a high team value then, as you progress through the season, you will invariably be able to afford a combination of players that perhaps others can't. However, I do not see deliberately building squad value as a viable strategy.

For starters, if you are having a successful campaign then you will naturally have players who are rising in price. If your focus is on getting your squad right, then increased team value should naturally come, but the price changes are affected by the transfer activity of the entire market. The transfers of the managers in the bottom eight million affect the price as much as the transfers from those in the Top 10k. Just because the crowd is doing it doesn't make it the right thing to do.

At the beginning of the season, in particular, the prices are incredibly volatile; they jump all over the place. This is one of the primary reasons people fall into the temptation of making early transfers, because they want to avoid a price rise (or price drop) which will adversely affect their team value.

I do not worry too much about team value. Your season is defined by Total Points at the end of GW38, not pounds in the squad/bank. It is certainly not an important enough factor to make an early transfer to the detriment of having all the possible information available. If you transfer in a premium asset at the beginning of the week, only to find out in the press conference at the end of the week that the player has picked up a long-term injury, then you have wasted two transfers, because you will be transferring him out for the next Gameweek.

CHIP STRATEGY

Chips were introduced to the game in the 2015/16 season.[16] Those who played the game back then may remember the All Out Attack chip, which allowed you to bench all three defenders during the Gameweek it was activated. This was quite underwhelming compared to the other two chips and was replaced prior to the 2017/18 season by the Free Hit chip.

Your chip strategy should be dynamic and adapt to the nuances of each season. In this section, I will provide a simple, five-step, guide on how to determine your own chip strategy but first, I will discuss each chip and how, generally speaking, I believe they fit into a typical season.

Free Hit (FH)

The Free Hit chip allows the manager to make unlimited free transfers to their squad for that Gameweek. Unlike the Wildcard (WC), the team will revert back to how it was in the Gameweek prior to the chip being played. I typically use my Free Hit to mitigate a points loss rather than to maximise points in any given Gameweek. There is always at least one big blank Gameweek in a season and sometimes more. This is normally caused by fixture congestion, matches postponed due to weather and clashes with domestic cup competitions.

I see lots of managers using their Free Hit in an early Gameweek because most of their players have difficult fixtures or are playing one another. This, to me, is a waste of the chip. Players can still haul on these Gameweeks and you are squandering a

[16] Chips can be used to (potentially) enhance your team's performance during the season. Only one chip can be used in a single Gameweek.

chip, which can be put to much better effect. I have seen managers who have been happy with their squad but have been so impacted by a blank Gameweek that they are only fielding five (playing) players of their 15-man squad.

If we imagine a semi-decent Gameweek score being 55, then on average each player will score five points. If you only had five of your 15-man squad playing, then you have six players missing. At five points per man, this is a 30-point deficit you could claw back by using your Free Hit at the right time.

Triple Captain (TC)

Ah, the bane of my life! With the exception of the 2021/22 season – when it didn't go too badly – I have had rotten luck with my Triple Captain chip. The Mané Double Gameweek Disaster I may have already brought up once or twice.[17]

Despite this – and this is where self-discipline is essential – I cannot, and will not, look past using this chip on a double Gameweek. A huge number of managers use this chip early in the season and/or in a normal Gameweek. It would be understandable for any manager who used their Triple Captain on Salah in the opening Gameweek of the 2020/21 season to take their 60-point return and tell me exactly what to do with my strategy; however, probability is against them.

Look at it this way: making one of your players your captain is equivalent to cloning one of your players and playing him, in an additional slot, again. Therefore, using your Triple Captain is effectively like cloning one of your players *twice* and fielding an *extra two* of him in a Gameweek. Instead of playing with 12

[17] Is it becoming obvious that this incident has left me with permanent mental scarring?

players (your normal 11 plus your "captain clone"), you are effectively playing with 13 players (your normal 11 plus an additional two of your captain clones). Using your Triple Captain chip on a player who is playing twice in a double Gameweek is like fielding 16 players (your normal captain, plus two captain clones, twice!). This may not lead to a favourable result, but the odds are clearly more stacked in your favour. If it goes wrong for you, then it is particularly unlucky.

It would be disingenuous for me not to mention that the risk of rotation is always increased in a double Gameweek, as the two games for that player are often close together. This risk can be mitigated somewhat by doing some quick research: is the player rotated often or is he a more nailed-on pick who rarely gets his minutes managed?

Bench Boost (BB)

The Bench Boost allows the points scored by all four bench players to count towards the Gameweek total. There is an extremely powerful way to play this chip but it must be combined with one of your two Wildcards and is dependent on how the rescheduled fixtures fall. Effectively, the strategy goes like this:

Imagine there is a big double Gameweek coming up, with lots of teams playing twice because (and this is important) they have already been omitted from an earlier blank Gameweek. The idea is that you play your Wildcard the week prior to this double Gameweek (because you can't play a Bench Boost AND your Wildcard in the same Gameweek) and make your entire 15-man squad from players who are in teams who play twice in the next double Gameweek. In the double Gameweek, you play your Bench Boost, *et voilà*. Each one of your 15-man squad is playing twice. You are playing with 30 players. If we go back to our example of an average Gameweek (each player scoring five points) then it is not unreasonable to expect a return of 150 points that Gameweek.[18]

A word of warning with this strategy is that it is very easy to get too focused on the double Gameweek. As with the initial squad selection, make sure that your squad makes sense in the games subsequent to the double Gameweek. It will be counterproductive if you gain lots of points in the double Gameweek only to lose them in the following weeks because your squad is weak.

In the 2020/21 season I ended up building my squad around DGW19 only to suffer fixture postponements through Covid-19 and had many players play only one of the two games. When I used my Wildcard in GW16, I set up my squad with 14 players who were playing twice, plus Heung-Min Son who was only playing once. Of my "29 players", six didn't play due to rearranged fixtures, three didn't play due to rotation and 15 of them blanked. I got 84 points when I was aiming for a minimum of 120. I was bitterly disappointed but, because I had played my Wildcard with the future in mind, I managed to claw my lost rank back with some big scores in the subsequent Gameweeks.

First Wildcard (WC1)

Wildcards are a powerful tool and should not be used lightly. Different seasons offer different challenges and opportunities so how I use my Wildcards will differ each season.

---

[18] It rarely works out like this, of course! If you want to temper your expectations then consider deducting 20% from your predicted total to cover injuries and rotation.

As a general rule, I try to keep my first Wildcard available until right at the end of the first half of the season (before I lose it). This is so that I can take advantage of fixture abnormalities or, in the absence of any, play it when I have as much player data as humanly possible to ensure my post-Wildcard squad has been backed by good knowledge.

If I do play my Wildcard early, my internal rule is that I will not play it any earlier than GW6. I think six Gameweeks is a period of time which offers a reasonable amount of data to enable managers to make an informed choice on their new squad. I see a lot of managers play their WC1 in GWs 3 to 5 – I believe this is because it is a very effective time to capture player value. While I myself feel the pull of this temptation, it is to be avoided. Please note: the temptation to use your Wildcard early on will be there even if you are doing well. If, like most managers, your rank is not where you want it to be in the opening weeks, the pull to use your Wildcard will be stronger. It is at this stage that you will have to summon immense willpower to resist clicking that button. But here's why you should resist:

At this stage of the season, you do not have enough useful data to base your transfer decisions on, which increases the likelihood that one of your most important tools goes to waste.

Consider a hypothetical example of someone who is playing their Wildcard ahead of GW4. They are strongly considering bringing in a player who hauled in the last game (GW3), and are looking to shift out a player who has disappointed in every game. Let's say this (desired) player got a modest return in GW1 and blanked in GW2. Naturally, all eyes are on that player for his GW3 haul, but what does this tell you? Almost nothing. After three Gameweeks, the player has respectively blanked, given an average return, and hauled. The only thing you can rely on here is that the player is probably first choice. As for forecasting future returns, there just isn't enough data. This player could go on to be a season keeper, inconsistent or a complete flop.

Let us delve deeper and imagine the player you are looking to shift out had a poor start (three consecutive blanks) but then hit his stride and went on to be a consistent source of points. You have brought in a player who, for all you know, is going to crash and burn, in exchange for a player who could go on to be one of the top performers of the season. You now have this exact same dilemma with your 14 other players. So, as well as your Wildcard probably not providing the squad turnaround you were hoping for, you now have no safety net for an injury crisis or for navigating blank and double Gameweeks. This will bite you later on.

Second Wildcard (WC2)

I always find the Second Wildcard a bit of a funny one and I have to admit I preferred it when there was only one. If you have held your nerve and played your First Wildcard nearer to the midway point then, assuming you played it to good effect, by the final third of the season you shouldn't have too strong a desire to reset your squad again, and therefore you should only need to use it for minor tweaks.

It can, however, be used to navigate the late-season blank and double Gameweeks or to capture a fixture swing. You can use it to maximise the number of players featuring in a double Gameweek or, if you've already used your Free Hit, you can construct, over time, a less than optimum double Gameweek team but one which features only players who are unaffected by a blank Gameweek. This team can then get you through the blank Gameweek and your Second Wildcard can be used to return your team to something more satisfactory.

As I said above, I like to combine a Wildcard with a Bench Boost on a double Gameweek. If you've got a late-season double Gameweek, this can be an explosive combo.

Using your Wildcard to capture player value

Many managers wait until the end of a Gameweek to play their Wildcard. While reasons for doing so are individual, usually this is because midweek events (injuries, rotation, standout performance) have provoked a sudden decision to play it. Other managers may have planned to target a particular Gameweek to play their Wildcard but are waiting on all the possible information before pulling the trigger. This is an admirable strategy, but managers who wait until right before the deadline are squandering a unique opportunity.

Earlier I discussed how deliberately focusing on team value as part of your transfer strategy is not, in my opinion, a worthwhile avenue to pursue. That does not mean, however, that team value is irrelevant. If you get a chance to capture player value without compromising more important elements then you should take it. Playing your Wildcard (either one) offers such an opportunity.

At the beginning of the 2021/22 season, I had noted a significant fixture swing around GW7. Chelsea had a rough start to the campaign, whereas Manchester United opened with a pleasant run of fixtures. Around GW7, this reversed. Manchester City, to a lesser degree, mimicked Chelsea's start with fixtures improving dramatically in GW8. Besides this, it was clear that Tuchel was still settling on his preferred XI and tactical system, having not yet had a full season as manager.

I earmarked this as a good place to play my first Wildcard which, following a slow start to the season, I did. The moment GW6 finished, I hit the Wildcard button. Instantly, I noted five of my transfer targets were due an overnight price rise. Two of my outgoing players were due a price drop. I made the transfers instantly and captured, in practical terms, £0.7m in team value. I took this further and brought in some players I was only considering. Why not? There was no downside to doing so. After all, if I changed my mind, or those players got injured, I could always move them on for someone else. By the end of the week, I had captured £1.1m in player value, simply by navigating the price changes in real time. Many other managers, who waited until the end of the week to play their Wildcard, failed to capture that value.

There is, however, an inherent danger to this and that is becoming *too* focused on player value. You may find yourself unwittingly drawn to those players who are due a price rise, ahead of those who are actually better picks. The same important part of your brain that enjoys earning money may bias your decisions towards players who will increase your team value. Making money is addictive even when it is merely a theoretical football budget. Be aware of this and make sure your Wildcard team is the one you believe will get you the most points, even if this means you lose a little bit of value.

Adapt your chip strategy to the season

The fixture chaos changes every year, and sometimes the double Gameweeks feature teams whose assets you are not keen on or who are playing difficult opposition twice, so your chip and Wildcard strategy should be adaptive each season.

The point of holding on to your chips/Wildcards is that you possess more tactical flexibility if you still have them in your arsenal. I will state, however, that if your team has been hit by an injury crisis, or you have got your team selection badly wrong and find a lot of your players are not first choice (or some combination of the two), then you need to use your judgement. I would not hesitate to use either Wildcard early if more than five of my players were injured or not being started.

Ben Crellin

This gentleman gets his own section, albeit a short one, because what he does for the FPL community is so valuable. In simple terms, Ben Crellin makes spreadsheets to help FPL managers navigate the footballing schedule each season. His spreadsheets are a vital source of information for forward planning chip strategy. His understanding of how the Premier League scheduling system works is incredible and, using this knowledge, he can accurately predict what is likely to happen before they make it official. His spreadsheets make it clear (with colour coding) what definitely will happen, what is very likely to happen or what is merely a possibility so that, as managers, we can exercise our own judgement and inform our own strategy. He is also happy to share his thoughts on how to navigate the chaos, and boasts a decent FPL record. Ben's most up-to-date spreadsheets can be found on his Twitter profile at https://twitter.com/BenCrellin.

Developing your own chip strategy in 5 steps

I see a lot of managers get incredibly frustrated with blank and double Gameweeks. Often those same people will demand answers to the question, "what is the best chip strategy?". Well, I am afraid there isn't a "best chip strategy"; there is only the optimal chip strategy for your team, at any given time. To work out what that is, you are going to have to do some deep thinking. Someone else, who has only taken a fleeting look at your squad, cannot answer the question for you and this is no small part because they will be biased by their own chip strategy, which may well be optimal for their team, but won't be for yours.

Here is my 5-step process on how to determine your own chip strategy. To assist in the explanation, I am going to take a working example from GW26 of the 2021/22 season. Here is a bit of background as to how things looked at that time.

Following the fixture postponement chaos, during the winter of 2021, the overlords at FPL Towers granted each manager a second Free Hit chip – the first time this had ever been done in the history of FPL. During this period there had been a handful of minor blank and double Gameweeks (for example when Chelsea attended, and won, the FIFA Club World Cup).

As we approached GW26, I still had all my chips (except for WC1) intact. GW26 was confirmed as the first major double gameweek of the season, with eight teams playing twice. It was also confirmed that in GW27, four teams were going to blank. Furthermore, we knew that due to the FA Cup quarter finals, we would have a big blank in GW30 with only three fixtures which could definitely go ahead, even though this had not yet been announced. Finally, there were still a lot of fixtures to reschedule from the aforementioned chaos – despite DGW26 – and there were only a limited number of places the Premier League schedulers could use to catch up, with the largest available gap being around GW33 and GW36; so it was fair to predict at least two more large double Gameweeks would take place there.

With that example in mind, here are the five steps to take when developing your own optimal chip strategy.

1. Know the schedule

Assuming you have managed to keep hold of your chips until the blank and double Gameweeks begin, the first thing you need to do is learn as much as you can about what the schedule does – and is *likely to* – look like.

Events can loosely be segregated into three categories: First, those fixtures which are confirmed and can therefore be relied upon. Second, there's what can reasonably be deduced even though it has not been confirmed. To take the above example: BGW30 was not officially guaranteed prior to GW26, but we knew which teams had progressed to the quarter finals of the FA Cup and when those matches were scheduled to take place. On that basis, we could reasonably assume when those teams would blank in the Premier League in order to accommodate the FA Cup fixtures. Then, finally, there is what we don't know, for example: if there are several fixtures still to be rescheduled, but there's no obvious period when this will happen.

2. Eliminate the variables

Once we know how the schedule is likely to look, we can start to eliminate the variables by assigning our chips to the future events we know are going to – or at least, highly likely to – take place. Using the above example: I knew that GW30 was going to be a huge blank gameweek with potentially only 6 out of the 20 teams featuring. Immediately, I earmarked one of my two Free Hit chips for this eventuality. In addition, and because I like to combine my Wildcard with a Bench Boost, I knew that I was going to save both (WC2 + BB) for the big double, which had to occur near the end of the season.

With three out of my five chips now earmarked for future events, I knew that my chip strategy for DGW26 had to be either using my Triple Captain chip or one of my two Free Hit chips.

3. Determine the critical factors and analyse your team with respect to them

Once the options are narrowed down, you then need to look at the upcoming Gameweeks in question, decide what is important and how your team fits around those aspects.

To use the above example, the following things stood out to me:

- GW26 featured eight teams who were playing twice – not an insignificant number of matches

- Liverpool and Arsenal, in particular, had two very nice fixtures for the double Gameweek

- With Salah having returned from AFCON, and Liverpool having such a great double, there probably wouldn't be a better opportunity to play the Triple Captain chip on a player

- In GW27, four teams were confirmed to blank, including Liverpool and Arsenal.

This was quite a tricky combination of variables because the assets you would want to target for GW26, then blanked in GW27. Also, by playing the Triple Captain chip on Salah, managers could not utilize the Free Hit chip to stock up on players who played twice. Conversely, by playing the Free Hit chip to "attack" the double Gameweek, we weren't able to play the Triple Captain chip on Salah, and hence would miss out on a golden opportunity.

It became clear to me that the optimal chip strategy at this juncture was incredibly dependent on how a manager's team was already set up. For me, I owned just two assets from Liverpool and Arsenal (which was uncommonly low) and only four assets who played twice. This put me at a disadvantage for GW26 (because I only had a few players playing twice) but at an advantage for GW27 (because I could easily navigate the blank gameweek without using a chip).

I decided that it would probably be better for me to use the Free Hit chip in GW26, rather than the Triple Captain chip on Salah. Had I, like many others, already owned lots of Liverpool and Arsenal assets, then I would have played the Triple Captain on Salah and used my Free Hit to get out of trouble when those teams blanked in GW27.

4. <u>Work out what you would do in each case</u>

Once your choices are narrowed down to a couple of possibilities, you should then work out what you would do in either scenario. Using the above example, I knew that if I played my Free Hit, I would field 11 players who played twice to really maximize my chances of generating a huge score. My focus would be on tripling up on Arsenal and Liverpool players, because they had the better fixtures, and then have a spread of players from the teams who played twice but whose fixtures weren't quite as good.

At the other end of the spectrum, I knew that I if were to play the Triple Captain chip on Salah, I would probably make a number of transfers to attack GW26 and use the Free Hit in GW27 to get out of trouble. That being said, my transfers would also have to look beyond DGW26 because, unlike with the Free Hit scenario, those players would be a permanent fixture in my team and, therefore, future fixtures would also need to be considered.

5. Input prediction figures for each scenario

When you know what you would do in each case, it is then a good idea to 'test run' both scenarios and for this you need to input some prediction data. This doesn't have to be rocket science; you just need some reasonable numbers to assign to each player. This is how I do it:

First, I assign five points to each player, per fixture. I feel this is a good halfway house between a player blanking and player getting a haul. Obviously, we don't know which ones will blank and which ones will haul, so I just apply the five points uniformly to each player. I then modify this figure based on fixture difficulty, so, for example, if the FDR is two, I add one point (making six). If the FDR is three, I leave it at five. If the FDR is four, I deduct one point (making four), and so on.

Once you have done this for each scenario, you get an idea of how many points you can reasonably assume you will get. If you are playing the Triple Captain chip then you should treat the player you are intending to captain differently from the rest of your players. After all, you must feel that this player can go above and beyond, otherwise you wouldn't waste a precious chip on him.

Using the above example, Salah was the standout choice for the Triple Captain chip. I looked at the fixtures (Norwich at home followed by Leeds at home) and decided it was not unreasonable to expect Salah to get a goal and an assist in each fixture (plus full BPS). I calculated that Salah would get 26 points over the two fixtures (that's 52 if he was captained and 78 if the TC chip was played).

Looking at my figures, I calculated that playing the Free Hit (and putting the armband on Salah) would earn me 160 points. Playing my Triple Captain would earn me 152 points. Therefore, playing the Free Hit would yield the better outcome, albeit by very little. I then looked at what would happen if Salah blanked in both games. In this situation I would earn 132 points Free Hitting as opposed to 110 points playing the Triple Captain. The worse Salah did, the better the outcome for me. In addition, I would still get to keep hold of my Triple Captain chip which can be effectively utilised in a gameweek where only one team doubles. On the other hand, a Free Hit – when used offensively – is at its most dangerous when used in a large double gameweek. This helped cement my decision.[19]

[19] As it happened Salah did haul in both games, scoring 28 points in the gameweek – slightly more than I had allowed for. Those who Triple Captained him earned 84 points. Despite this, and because my Free Hit was so successful, I earned 150 points, beating the majority of managers who played their Triple Captain chip, whilst retaining my own (which, it must be said, was subsequently wasted!).

DEADLINES

This might seem incredibly basic, but you would not believe the number of managers I have witnessed hurting themselves by missing deadlines. Particularly since the advent of Friday night matches and, even worse, Friday night early kick-offs.[20]

Once a Gameweek is over, the first thing you should do is find out exactly how long you have got to make your next transfer(s). Set a reminder if you think you will forget.

I am an advocate of waiting as long as possible before making a transfer, apart from in certain scenarios (covered later), but if you are going to be waylaid (work, child's birthday party, tap-dancing lesson) then ensure you make your changes prior to the latest opportunity.

[20] Both of which have been testing my marriage.

SUBSTITUTES' BENCH

The use of the bench is a subject of disagreement amongst many FPL managers and, broadly, people's attitude towards the bench falls into one of three categories:

Squad depth is important

Managers who go with this mantra opt for a very well-balanced team, with all three substitute positions occupied by someone who is likely to play.

The sort of manager who adopts this viewpoint will be very resilient to injury crises. If everyone on your bench is likely to play, then you will need more than four injuries (if you use your free transfer) before your starting XI haemorrhages points.

The downside is that it will spread your budget more thinly across your squad, meaning you will have less money to indulge in higher-scoring premium assets.

Second, and important from a psychological perspective, these managers are more prone to having wasted points on their bench when they get the rotation wrong (which, trust me, they will).

Just for fun, here is a table showing Tomas Soucek's point returns between GW15 and GW22 in the 2020/21 season and whether or not he was in my starting XI.

GW	Points	Status
15	10	Didn't own
16	3	Transferred in with WC1, starting XI
17	11	Bench

18	Blank GW	Transferred out on FH
19	2 + 2	Starting XI (DGW)
20	15	Bench
21	1	Starting XI
22	9	Bench

While this may frustrate beyond belief, I take comfort in knowing I have safety on the bench. There is nothing more satisfying than a big score coming off your bench to cover a player who unexpectedly doesn't play.

Only 11 players score points

At the opposite end of the spectrum, there are those managers who will seek to maximise output from the starting XI and so will pick the cheapest possible players to occupy the bench. More often than not, the very cheapest players are priced accordingly because they don't stand a cat in hell's chance of starting.

This is a powerful strategy for generating points because the budget is well spent on the starting XI. The obvious downside is that this sort of manager could experience the odd very painful Gameweek if they are hit by injury or rotation.

Depth is good, but the third spot is a waste

Some managers take a more balanced approach and ensure their first and second spots are well covered but will effectively sacrifice the third spot to inject more cash into the starting XI.

This isn't a dangerous strategy because it is quite rare that you will call upon your third substitute, although it happens. Often people who plan to play five in midfield will buy the cheapest striker they can find who will effectively rot in the third spot, thus freeing up funds to be spent elsewhere.

My approach

I use a more adaptive strategy, which changes between 1 and 3 depending on the stage the season is at.

At the very start of the season, I adopt a more cautious approach. There will be shocks with who is first choice and perhaps even (real-life) transfers or loan deals will occur, once the football has kicked off. Therefore, at the start of the season, the risk profile is higher and hence I adopt an approach closer to number 1, where I make sure my bench is well equipped.

Approaching GWs 5 and 6, the dust settles. The picture of who is first choice is much clearer, and the initial squad issues have been resolved. From here, I will move more to a number 3 stance. I always like to have some cover so I never go as far as number 2.

As we approach GWs 10–12, and the busy Christmas schedule looms, I think about getting squad depth back again. This does not mean to say that I prioritise my bench over more pressing matters, but it is certainly on my radar and may influence short-term thinking.

By GWs 13–15, I want my bench to be full of players who I know are going to play.

When the busy fixture schedule calms down, I will then revert to a number 3 mentality until the end of the season, except for when utilising my Bench Boost.

THE FINAL GAMEWEEKS

The very end of a season can be another turbulent time for FPL managers. If it has been a tight season, then you may find that there are many teams at the top of the table who still have a lot to play for, be it to win the title or qualify for European football. The teams in (or around) the relegation zone should be fighting for their lives. Quite often teams in a relegation battle have a big performance surge at the end of the campaign because they need to show true character and grit to turn results around in their bid to stay up.

Aside from this, there will always be those teams who are locked into mid-table obscurity. The ones who don't have much to aim for (because European football is too far out of sight), nor are they overly afraid of relegation (because they are suitably far ahead). These teams may drop off a bit because they have lost motivational energy; performances may suffer as a result. Managers (real-life ones) may take this opportunity to give youth or fringe players a run-out, thus increasing the risk of first-team rotation.

In some seasons, a team may get mathematically relegated or secure a European spot with quite a few games left to play, in which case the same thing might happen. Therefore, towards the very end of a season, I tend to go back to having a strong bench. Likewise, this can be a bad time to play your chips or Wildcard.

There is always a temptation to hold on to your chips until the very last moment, so if you are neck and neck with a rival, or on the fringes of your desired rank tier, you can pull away at the last moment, like a sprinter giving their last burst of energy at the finish line. I've witnessed many managers (myself included) use a Bench Boost and/or a Free Hit in the last couple of Gameweeks of a season, only to find that several players were rotated or lacked drive.

It is always better to play it during the Gameweeks where the maximum gain can be achieved, even if that means rivals will hold their chips over you for the rest of the season.

NAVIGATING FIXTURE POSTPONEMENTS

I wrote the First Edition of this book during the 2020/21 season when Covid changed our lives for ever and caused unprecedented disruption to the footballing campaign. Little did we know at the time that this was to be nothing compared to the complete chaos that Covid would cause during the 2021/22 season.

It is fair to assume that Covid and its variants will be something which we will have to live with for a long time. Even if we defeat Covid – assuming it is truly possible to do so – we may find another virus or highly contagious disease appears in its wake. While this may seem a very gloomy outlook, I feel it necessary to share some of the hard lessons I have learned while trying to navigate Covid during the last two seasons.

First and foremost, Covid is indiscriminate and random. When the Omicron variant went tearing through Premier League teams during the winter of 2021/22 it did so with no discernible pattern. The identity of the players who had tested positive was (generally) kept confidential by the clubs and, in some cases, fixture postponements were being announced within a couple of hours of the match kicking off. These factors made it almost impossible to navigate the FPL landscape with any degree of certainty. It also meant that the ever-present luck factor played a much greater part in the fortunes of managers who were disproportionally affected depending on which players/teams were randomly struck down.

Despite this, there are a number of practical steps you can take to minimise the risk to your squad during Covid or any other crisis which is causing fixture postponements in the Premier League.

Information is key; do not make early transfers

I am not an advocate of early transfers in normal times, although, as you will discover later, there are circumstances in which I am willing to make an exception. When Covid is prevalent, however, there is never a worse time to make early transfers.

Even if it is looking likely that you will be priced out of your desired transfer, my advice is firmly this: find another option. The number of people I have seen making transfers midweek, only to hear in the Friday press conference that a particular player is now self-isolating, having returned a positive Covid test, is unbelievable. I have seen those managers raging on social media and bemoaning their bad luck. This is not bad luck. This is the (highly likely) outcome of their impatience.

In a season afflicted by Covid, you will have your fair share of bad luck. Do not add to your own misery by making any moves before every scrap of information is available. This means waiting until the very end of the Gameweek before finalising your transfers. The merest hint of a Covid outbreak in a club's training facility should be enough to make you re-consider transferring in players who are taking part in that club's corresponding fixture. Even if it means losing £0.1m value on your player, hold your horses and wait until the deadline.

Do not leave it too late to make your transfers

I know this sounds contradictory after reading the above, but allow me to explain.

In GW19 of the 2021/22 season, Covid had already devastated the schedule and was continuing to cause problems, with new breakouts being reported all over the Premier League. Training grounds were being closed. Dozens of senior players were testing positive. Teams were requesting postponements.

In the previous Gameweek, I – and many others – suffered a most unfortunate blow when, after transferring in two Aston Villa players ahead of their fixture with Burnley, the match was postponed less than two hours before the Gameweek deadline. This was a bitter pill to swallow.

With this still fresh in everyone's minds, many FPL managers waited until the very end of the Gameweek deadline before hitting the button. The logic of this could not be disputed. Unfortunately, due to the unusually high web traffic this extra caution was causing, the Official FPL website could not handle the spike in activity and the server crashed roughly five minutes before the cut-off point.

This incident affected managers to varying degrees. Some managers' transfers came through as intended. Others missed the deadline altogether and ended up accidentally rolling forward a free transfer. But those who were most severely punished were the ones who had made transfers with the intention of playing their Free Hit chip.[21] Many of these managers found that while their transfers had gone through, the activation of their chip hadn't. One FPL account I saw posted a screenshot of their team after the deadline. They had scored 102 points but, because their Free Hit remained inactive during

---

[21] If you play your Wildcard or Free Hit chip then any points deductions from transfers already made in that Gameweek are totally wiped out. As a result of this managers will often deliberately make the transfers at a points cost, knowing that the deductions will be removed once they play the chip.

the server crash, the 27 transfers that the Free Hit represented went through at a cost of 104 points. This meant that, despite having an absolutely stunning Gameweek, this particular FPL manager was rewarded with a Gameweek score of –2 points!

It is important to learn from this. Leaving your transfers to the last minute is strongly advisable but leaving it *too* late could be devastating. I would therefore recommend hitting the "Confirm transfers" button no less than 30 minutes before the deadline to avoid getting caught out by high traffic on the server.

Avoid double-ups/triple-ups

As discussed earlier in the book, I generally advise against too many double/triple-ups in pre-season, but then relax this rule as the season progresses. During a Covid-affected season, however, it is worth going back to basics and spreading the risk across your squad.

In GW18 of the 2021/22 season, six out of the ten matches were postponed. Including those on my bench, I managed to field just six players that Gameweek and there were those who were even more unfortunate than I was.

If you have tripled-up on players from two teams – which is not uncommon – then you could end up losing six players from a single fixture postponement. Even the most well-staffed of benches cannot cope with that.

Have your C and VC on players from different fixtures

During the 2021/22 season, I would frequently captain Mo Salah and assign vice-captain to Trent Alexander-Arnold whenever

Liverpool had a decent fixture. If, for some reason, Salah didn't play, I would put my trust in Trent to come up with the goods.

While this captaincy strategy is perfectly sensible, it must be avoided when Covid is rampant. You should also avoid having your vice-captaincy set on a player from the opposing team of the same fixture (although, arguably, this would be uncommon practice anyway). To lose players from a match postponement is painful. To lose the chance to score double points from your captain would be enough to make you tear your own eyeballs out.

Have a strong bench

This one speaks for itself. During the Covid crisis in the winter of 2021/22, I required the use of all three bench players five Gameweeks in a row (between GW17 and GW21). Even then, my bench did not cover my starting XI losses.

Not having a strong bench during Covid times can be season suicide.

Be wary of rotation/injury-prone players

Sometimes you get those annoying players who have a really high points-ceiling – that is to say are as likely to haul as they are to return – but who are also prone to rotation or injury. This means you have to offset their returns potential with the fact that they may get reduced minutes. Phil Foden is a fantastic example of this. While it is annoying when a player such as this gets zero minutes, I often feel it is worth it for the points they acquire when they do play, especially if you can mitigate the risk with a strong bench.

It goes without saying that during a Covid-hit season, these sorts of players will only add to your misery. When all the players on your bench are being called up due to fixture postponements, the last thing you want is a bunch of players who are regularly rotated/injured.

GOLDEN RULE #2:

Do not take points hits (unless it is absolutely necessary to do so[22])

I know this Golden Rule will be a controversial one but I loathe points hits; I really do. To me, they represent the ultimate evil temptation in the game. I want to make it clear from the outset that many successful managers regularly employ points hits as part of their strategy, but my feeling is managers end up worse off overall when they take regular hits.

The consensus in the FPL community seems to be that they are only to be taken with caution, that the occasional points hit is fine as long as you don't overdo it. The trouble is, how many times is occasional? What is overdoing it? When is it all right to take a points hit and when is it not? For me personally, I will only consider a points hit in the following situations:

1. When I have several injuries which my bench won't cover and do not have a Wildcard to play. This is because the outgoing transfers are guaranteed to get me zero points.

2. When there is a blank or double Gameweek which has caught me off guard and *not* taking action will lead to falling behind, or missing out on an excellent opportunity.

3. If I am desperately chasing rank and find my team is totally inappropriate for making the rank gains required.

Even in the above situations, I do not do it lightly.

[22] Remember, we have to be adaptable!

There are two ways to look at points hits, and the lens through which you view them will have a bearing on whether you believe they are a viable ongoing strategy.

The first way to look at it is what I call the *gross effect* of taking a points hit. In simple terms, it goes like this:

- I transferred in Player A and Player B for a –4 hit
- Player A got 3 points
- Player B got 4 points
- Total = 7 points
- 7 – 4 = 3
- After my 4-point hit, I am left with 3 points (from the 7), therefore my points hit was justified

However, there are two sides to this coin. To transfer *in* two players, you must have transferred *out* two players.

This is when you look at the *net effect* of taking the hit. Or, to put it another way, what *would* have happened had you done nothing? Which often looks like this:

- I transferred in Player A and Player B for a –4 hit
- I transferred out Player Y and Player Z
- Player A got 3 points
- Player B got 4 points
- Total = 7 points
- 7 – 4 = 3

- Player Y and Player Z both blanked, only getting 2 points each simply for playing. Now the equation looks like this:
- 7 – 4 = 3
    - (Player A & B's score – the points hit = Gross Points)
- 3 – (2 – 2) = -1
    - (Gross Points – Player Y & Z's score = Net Points)
- The net effect is that I have lost 1 point. Doing nothing, in this case, was the optimal solution

Even though the players transferred out both blanked and the players brought in both did better, the best option in terms of *net gain* that Gameweek would have been to do nothing. This is why points hits are a dangerous business; they can lead people to believe they have made the right decision when exercising patience would have improved their overall score.

Regular points hitters reading this will be jumping up and down in their seat, screaming that there is a flaw to this argument, so I will address it. People do not take points hits just for that Gameweek. They do it with the future in mind, and so the effectiveness needs to be evaluated over time. But that argument works both ways.

Earlier we talked about keeping faith in your choices and with your squad. Often the game works in such a way that by having to put out fires elsewhere we get the benefit of huge hauls from players who we were desperate to transfer out only yesterday. Having one free transfer per week forces us to keep faith in players who we are unsure about. There have been so many occasions where I have had a thought along the lines of:

"Wow! He got me 12 points this week and I've been trying to get rid of him!"

Patience is often rewarded in FPL; however, points hits are a way of short-circuiting this natural safeguard. If you play the game in such a way that you are happy to take –4, –8 or even –12 points hits regularly, then the natural mechanism for forcing patient play goes out of the window.

This is one of those things which can have a really strong upside if you get it spot on, but again luck plays an enormous factor in this and, more often than not, you will get this wrong. Not necessarily because it was the wrong decision, but because the FPL Gods were not smiling on that particular player in that particular Gameweek.

I became somewhat fascinated with points hits in the 2019/2020 season and started recording the effectiveness of my own hits. Interested by the results, I recorded points hits I saw other managers taking and eventually recorded a season's worth of observations. What I noted was that, overall, the net position of managers across the season was that they suffered a significant loss. This was particularly true for those who took points hits in single Gameweeks and in early Gameweeks. Those who transferred out injured players for players who were playing twice in a double Gameweek fared much better, but not always.

Some people argue that taking points hits makes them feel better about their squad, and that it is worth it on that basis alone. If this is the case, then that is a fair justification to do it. As we will explore in the Psychology section, the most important thing is to enjoy playing FPL. If spending points to get your squad just how you want it helps you enjoy the game more, then go ahead.

If, however, your primary motivation is your overall points/rank at the end of a season, then I genuinely don't think that points hits are the way forward.[23]

***

Everything covered thus far will take you in a nice, circular loop from the end of one season, into pre-season preparation, and right the way through the next season. However, there are still a few things to discuss.

Importantly, what you have just read is all about <u>how I play</u> the game. After 18 years of getting things right and getting things wrong, I have carved out a way of playing the game which is exclusive to me. A way which aligns with my personality, stops me from having sleepless nights and has been shaped by my own unique experiences.

You and I may be very different from one another, and what keeps me up at night with worry may be exactly the thing which makes FPL enjoyable for you (and vice versa). It is therefore necessary to explore some of the different playing styles which are common amongst managers whom I have interacted with over the years.

[23] There is an excellent book written on this topic called *Fantasy Premier League – Taking A Hit: The Key to Success* by Paul Rogers. While the book doesn't arrive at quite the same conclusion as I do, it is, nevertheless, the most comprehensive study of points hits ever written.

PART 3:
PLAYING STYLES

During my rather varied career, I did a brief stint working in the banking industry. There I met a colleague called Dan O'Reilly. He has since become a close friend, although we no longer work together. Dan started playing FPL in the 2013/14 season, the year before we met, and I was pleased to meet a colleague who was already involved in the game. We created a work mini-league and it surprised me when he beat me that year. The season after that, I beat him (but not by much) and felt the universal balance had been restored. He then went on to beat me several years in a row and earned himself the title of my "FPL Nemesis".

These days I am in over a dozen mini-leagues, but there is one mini-league which continually comes into focus. Within that league, there is one name I am interested in, above all others: Dan O'Reilly. This man frustrates me more than I can convey with words. My FPL rivalry with him borders on obsession. I know *his* team almost as well as I know my own. I take great pleasure in his misfortunes and wince when one of his players hauls. When I am celebrating a great Gameweek result in front of my wife, she will often ask me: "But how did Dan do this week?"

What really annoys me about Dan is that he does things which make absolutely no sense to me. Don't get me wrong, he is a *proper* FPL player. He doesn't make silly mistakes like missing deadlines, or not realising there's an upcoming blank Gameweek, but his playing style is totally alien to me. It seems to be quite haphazard, yet simultaneously well thought out. He is gut-driven but seems to really interrogate his own thought processes. He takes punts which seem illogical, but quite often pay off, and will occasionally captain obscure players while ignoring the obvious picks. More importantly, he has reached a point where he beats me most seasons (although I am starting to pull things back my way now).

Frankly, I hate him.[24]

***

There are many different playing styles in FPL, and these can be drilled down and down to the level of the individual. It is therefore with great care that one tries to lump these into categories. But, for the sake of highlighting differing playing styles, I have created six main categories which I have observed over my FPL career.

In this section I try to identify certain traits present in these styles of play, the advantages which can be gained from playing that way, and highlight any dangerous aspects which are inherent in that playing style.

[24] He is godfather to my daughter, so clearly I don't hate him but I still want to wring his neck!

THE NUMBERS MANAGER

Stats-driven, the numbers manager will sift through mountains of data to guide their transfer and captaincy decisions.

The volume of data available to us these days is unreal. In football, platforms such as Opta Sports record an obscene number of statistics right down to how many times a player touched the ball in a match, how many of those touches were in the box, and so on. There are services and websites out there which will organise these stats and present them in a fashion which is more relevant to FPL. A lot of these services filter the data into Key Stats, usually defined as Shots, Shots on Target (SoT), Shots in the Box, Big Chances (BC) and Big Chances Created (BCC). Aside from these, there are three very popular metrics which are important to highlight:

Expected Goals (xG)

Opta Sports analyses every goalscoring opportunity a player has had in a game. This process begins when a player takes a shot (at the moment his foot strikes the ball) and gives the shot an xG rating. The shot is rated irrespective of whether or not it leads to a goal.

The higher the xG rating, the greater the possibility that the same shot would hypothetically result in a goal. Conversely, a lower xG rating means that the same hypothetical shot would be less likely to result in a goal.

Opta Sports compare each shot taken to a vast database containing hundreds of thousands of shots. The database contains shots from a multitude of distances, angles and situations to create the xG metric. It treats the value of the shot on its own merit, in every situation, and so does not take into account differences in player ability (for example, in the exact same situation, Lionel Messi and Glenn Murray would get the same xG rating).

The xG value assigned to a given shot is based on many factors. The big one is distance from goal: the closer to goal the shot is, the higher the xG. It analyses the angle(s) available to the player from the ball to the goal (taking into account if there is a goalkeeper and/or defenders blocking the shot). If the opportunity is defined as a Big Chance by Opta Sports, then this will increase the xG rating. There are other, smaller, metrics which fine tune the xG such as whether the player was under pressure when he was taking the shot and if the ball was travelling towards the goal when it was struck. It is quite detailed.

So a tap-in from three yards out, with the goalkeeper face down on the deck, could give an xG of, say, 0.95. This means that in a situation like this, 95 times out of 100, a player will convert that opportunity into a goal. If a player strikes a volley from outside the box, with a wall of defenders in front of him, that could give an xG of around, say, 0.10, meaning that only 10% of shots like that will result in a goal.

Expected Assists (xA)

Expected Assists uses a similar model to that which calculates xG, only it focuses on the creation of a chance.

It measures the probability that a pass or a cross will result in a direct assist but is fine-tuned to the type of pass, where the pass was made, and if it found its recipient in space. Again, it is not necessary for a goal to be scored for xA to be awarded.

Expected Goal Involvement (xGI)

The third key metric, xGI is a combination of xG and xA. It measures the expectation of a player to score a goal, or create an assist during key stages in the games they have played. This can be a powerful tool when analysing a player's potential to generate FPL points.

How should these metrics be used?

To put it simply, with caution.

For statistics which are widely used, they contain something of a paradox when applying them practically.

First, a player with a high xGI is clearly getting in all the right places. Depending on his position, he is creating or receiving good opportunities, irrespective of anything else. This can help identify players who may not show up on the "recent form" radar but have been performing well.

Second, it is useful to compare a player's xGI to their actual goal involvement. This will give you a new metric, which is how a player is performing against his own xGI.

For example, if a forward has an xG of 15 but has scored 20 goals, then that player is **over-performing** against his xG. He is scoring more than he probably should, considering the quality of the opportunities he has had.

If a player has an xG of 10 but has only scored five goals, then he is **under-performing** against his xG. Given the quality of the opportunities he has had, he should really have scored more goals. In the above example, he should have scored twice as many goals as he did.

The problem is that it is possible to read this situation in two ways:

- An over-performing player is clinical with his finishing and scoring difficult opportunities that others would miss. I should get him in my team.
- An over-performing player is scoring at an unsustainable rate. He has been fortunate with the goals he has scored. Probability dictates that his goal rate will soon come down against his xG, so I should not get him in my team. I have probably missed the boat with this player.

Conversely:

- An under-performing player is getting in all the right spaces and creating good opportunities for himself to score, but he has been unlucky. His time will come, so I will get him in my team now because probability dictates that he will start converting these good opportunities soon.
- An under-performing player is getting good opportunities to score but just isn't a good finisher. Yes, he's getting in all the right places, but he can't convert his chances so I shouldn't get him in my team.

What this shows is that the practical implications of this data can often be contradictory and therefore must be used in tandem with *actually watching the players play*, evaluating their performance and using your own judgement.

Did the player miss the sitter because he was unlucky or because he can't finish his dinner at the moment? Was there a slight bobble on the ball as it reached his feet, or did he just spoon it over? These are the important nuances which you cannot read from stats alone.

NPxG+xA/90 – one stat to rule them all

If I have to focus on one stat, it is this one: NPxG+xA/90 – otherwise known as Non-Penalty Expected Goals plus Expected Assists per 90 minutes – is a compound metric which I find to be the most reliable.

Essentially, it is the total of a player's xG from all shots, excluding penalties, combined with their xA.[25] This creates a metric which measures goal involvement in general rather than looking at either statistic in isolation. This combined stat is then expressed as a ratio of minutes played – thus preventing players who have suffered from injury being penalised during the time they were absent.

I find it to be one of the purest and therefore most useful stats around when assessing goal involvement for attacking defenders, midfielders and forwards.

How you then use this information is totally personal. I find expected stats get more useful the further into the season you go, as the data pool gets larger. I know others who prefer to focus on more recent form and hence will look at a limited period of stats behind that Gameweek, say four to eight Gameweeks before. If you choose to use the former, then you need to be aware of any large-scale changes which may have

[25] All penalties share the same characteristics and hence have an xG of somewhere between 0.75 and 0.80 (at the time of writing and depending on who is recording the stats). Since the penalty awarded may have had nothing to do with the player who takes the penalty it is argued that the nominated penalty taker does not have the "right" to the xG, as they may not have contributed to the creation of the opportunity.

happened to the player, or his team, which could have caused those stats to become skewed. For example, you may find that a fall in a player's xGI correlates with a positional change, or the deployment of a new formation. In these cases, the expected stats prior to this event hold less weight because the circumstances in which they were generated are no longer relevant.

Bookies' odds

Bookies earn a living by using a wealth of data and statistics to calculate the probability of events and reeling in the money of punters who "fancy those odds". If they overstate the odds, they will lose too much money if the bet comes off. If they understate the odds, too few people will put money on it happening (or not happening).

The art form, therefore, is getting the odds of an event occurring *just* right. It is always worth having a glance at the bookies' odds for various things to help inform your transfer decisions, as the statistics will have been well and truly analysed to provide the most accurate probability.

I will have a glance at the bookies' odds, but they don't hold too much sway over my decision-making process. If I am really torn between two players, and all other comparisons are inconclusive, then the bookies' odds might help tip me over the edge.

***

Stats are an excellent tool to help assist the decision-making process, but they shouldn't be used as a replacement for everything else. Numbers don't lie, and as a result there is always the temptation to hide behind them and give them too strong a weighting. Sometimes you will get a powerful urge to make a certain move, and often this is your inner sense guiding you to a good decision. Just because the stats do not back up your gut feeling does not mean you shouldn't go with it.

Looking back to the spreadsheet I used in the 2014/15 season, I became so preoccupied with numbers that I became blind to the poor decisions I was walking into.

THE EYE-TEST MANAGER

An avid watcher of the game, the eye-test manager doesn't need stats to tell them who is the next big thing. They rely on what they see with their own eyes.

There is a lot to be said for this approach. As highlighted above, there are many ways in which statistics can be deceiving. There is no substitute for watching a game and picking up all the little details which the stats can't possibly tell you.

I remember seeing Riyad Mahrez for the first time when he played for Leicester City at the beginning of the 2015/16 season. I can't remember which game I saw him in, but I watched it in full, followed by highlights of the same game afterwards on *Match of the Day*. He didn't score, but watching his movement on, and off, the ball instantly made him my transfer target for that week. I just had the strong feeling that with that sort of ability and pace, it wouldn't really matter who he played, there was the chance of a points return and, besides, he only cost £5.5m. I was heavily rewarded for getting him in early – he hauled 240 points that season.

Of course, there is a great downside for the eye-test manager and that is time. Most of us have to leave the house once or twice a day in order to work, see friends or get the groceries in. Many of us have children who absorb a great deal of our time.

If you want to watch all 90 minutes of ten Premier League games, every weekend, then you will need to commit 15 hours a week to watching football. This is a commitment which most of us are unable to make. Realistically, we will be able to watch *some* of the matches. Maybe even half of the matches, if we have an understanding (or football-mad) partner. This is where the dilemma begins.

If your decision-making is largely based on what you see with your own eyes, but you are only watching half (being generous) of the matches each week, then the data you are relying on becomes skewed. You will make decisions based on what you have seen, and omit important data which you have missed. At least with statistics you get the total view of all players so the comparisons are fair.

To use my example above, if I had watched a different game to the Leicester one, I probably would not have brought in Mahrez when I did, and my season could have looked quite different.[26]

[26] I finished in the Top 70k that season.

THE RISK-AVERSE MANAGER

Preferring stability to short-term explosive returns, the risk-averse manager plays the long game and makes sensible, if not exciting, decisions.

I am a self-confessed risk-averse manager and have found my trajectory moving more in this direction as time has passed. Whenever I make a transfer, it is quite often not with the next Gameweek in mind. At any given stage of a season, I have a vision for how my team is going to look and I slowly and painfully etch out my team to synchronise with my vision, one free transfer at a time. I quite often will roll a free transfer just to buy myself an extra week's worth of data, to ensure I still want to make the decision.

Risk-averse managers tend not to take punts on unproven players. They abhor points hits, favour a deep squad with cover on the bench and will wait for a bandwagon to prove fruitful before jumping on it themselves. They save their chips like squirrels, stocking up for the cold winter months. The nature of FPL is long term and you will often hear the clichéd phrase "it's a marathon, not a sprint." In that sense, being averse to risks is no bad thing.

A major advantage with being risk-averse is that you are more likely to acquire what I deem 'accidental' points, that is to say, points from players who most people have lost patience with – and perhaps even taken a points hit to remove. It can be very satisfying when, instead of transferring out a player who is blanking (like everyone else seems to be), you instead focus on replacing an injured player, only to find the player who you were considering getting rid of, bags a 12-pointer.

The problem is, I have found that being risk-averse favours those who are already in a good situation. Whenever I have needed to push on from a low-rank situation, or I have had a really bad start to the season, my risk-averse nature holds me back from making the aggressive gains needed to end up with a big finish. I am much more of a "shield" than a "sword" sort of manager. However, employing the shield over the sword will not get you anywhere if you have had a bad start to the season and are ranked 3m or lower. In FPL, when you get stuck in a rut, it usually requires riskier measures (and a large dollop of luck) to get you out of it.

THE POINTS-CHASING MANAGER

Mega hauls every week, no matter the cost.

The ethos of the points-chasing manager is to treat every Gameweek like its own miniature campaign, with one goal in mind: maximise the points return and snap up exciting opportunities before anyone else does.

Unlike the risk-averse manager, the points-chaser goes out big and bold and, in general, their decision-making strategy will be limited to the one or two Gameweeks in front of them. They will not be shy about taking points hits to bring in a player who they believe is going to return big.

This type of manager will probably have a low-value bench and thus will project the largest amount of money on the starting XI. They are more likely to respond quickly to player bandwagons – often they are the ones who start them – and therefore boast huge team values which become helpful for future transfer decisions. Having a high team value can often mean being able to squeeze in an extra premium player later on.

They are more likely to seize opportunities, and hence you may find they often play their chips and Wildcards early in a season because they have spotted a chance they cannot resist or because they are determined to get out of a situation they dislike, as quickly as possible.

As a naturally risk-averse manager, I would find it stressful to play like this week in and week out. There are few points-chasers who get the risky calls right most of the time, over a 38-Gameweek season, and hence a great deal of "taking the rough with the smooth" is required for this style of play.

I would also say that this style is very difficult to maintain over several seasons and consistently get good results. This sort of manager is likely to have a varied FPL career history, finishing in the Top 10k one season and 1m the next year.

In stark contrast to the risk-averse manager, this style of aggressive play can see struggling managers make huge rank jumps in just a few Gameweeks, but it is laden with danger for those who already have a high overall rank.

If you are two-thirds of the way through the season, find yourself in the Top 10k and continue to make rash decisions, eventually you are going to have a catastrophic Gameweek, while other, more cautious managers are protecting their overall rank with sensible decisions. It is also more likely that those managers, with whom you are now competing, have all their chips still intact whereas you used yours much earlier. When things might be neck and neck, the other managers will have an advantage over you.

There is also a style of play which is known as Upside Chasing, which I, perhaps incorrectly, see as a combination of the Points-Chasing and Numbers playing styles.

In simple terms Upside Chasing is a method of play which means always picking the option with the best chance of a points haul, even if that means forgoing an option who is highly owned, or transferring out a premium asset who is not doing badly. This involves trusting your own judgement and, in doing so, sometimes going against the grain. High risk, high reward.

THE RULES-BASED MANAGER

A manager with a clear vision and strategy but who knows all too well the temptations of the game which could steer them off course.

Some managers create rules and systems which help govern their own transfer policy or simply to make the game more enjoyable for themselves (covered later).

These are managers who know exactly how they wish to conduct themselves throughout a campaign and will ensure their own vision is realised, even in difficult times, by creating firm rules which prevent them from succumbing to temptation.

An example of a rule-based system is Eric Freeman's "Lock and Swap" strategy.[27] In simple terms, this strategy involves selecting five premium players who are "locked", which means you have to put your faith in them for the entire season. Your transfers are therefore focused on your medium and budget-tier players, who need to be "swapped" based on form and fixtures in order to maximise their potential.

This is presented as a guide to reach 2,500 points, a self-confessed lofty ambition by the author; however, Eric makes a convincing numerical argument to justify this achievement.

Rules-based systems can be an effective way of ensuring a strategy is consistently implemented through the peaks and troughs of a season. It is a good way of stopping the psychological wheels falling off when you have three consecutive bad Gameweeks. There are, however, two things to be aware of:

---

[27] His article "A Guide to 2500 Points | The Lock and Swap Strategy" can be found on the Fantasy Football Hub website. It is definitely worth a read.

First, the success of a rules-based system is only as good as the rules which are imposed. If you had a rules-based strategy which, for example, said that your captain choice should always be one with less than 5% ownership and you must rotate your goalkeeper every week, you shouldn't expect a decent finish no matter how diligently you stick to the system.

Second, a rules-based system is only effective if you maintain it throughout the season. Imagine you are an omnipotent ghost watching an FPL manager. You know that one of their premium players has blanked five times in a row but, because you are an all-knowing, future-seeing ghost, you also know that same player is going to make three double-digit hauls. Only a rules-based system is going to stop that manager (unless they are incredibly patient) from transferring their blanking premium asset out for one who is returning. But it will only work if they keep their faith in the system and don't deviate from it. But herein lies a vulnerability.

Almost every season throws up an anomaly, something unique to that season. This happens to be one of the things I love about FPL.

- With the 2018/19 season, it was the emergence of attacking full backs as valuable FPL assets.
- In 2020, the season was suspended because of Covid-19, and everything we knew about FPL went out of the window with Project Restart.
- With the 2020/21 season major rule changes regarding interpretation of handballs led to a tremendous increase in the number of penalties given (although this tailed off towards the end of the season). Over the winter period,

the second wave of Covid-19 created even more disruption than it had in the previous season.

- During the 2021/22 season we saw a huge decrease in the number of points obtained from forwards, including premium ones.

Depending on the rules imposed, a rules-based strategy could prevent a manager from adapting to a season's abnormalities. If your strategy dictates that all your defenders must be less than £5m, how will you maximise returns in a season when premium defenders are returning much more than equivalently priced midfield and forward options?

If your strategy demands that your bench is to be populated by the lowest possible value assets, how will your squad cope with the increased demands of a season where something like Covid-19 is prevalent?

If I had implemented the Lock and Swap strategy in the 2020/21 season, I would have been stuck with Aubameyang until I played my Wildcard in GW16. The thought of that makes me shudder.

Since writing this, I have spoken with Eric Freeman and we discussed his strategy. Eric told me that, for better or worse, he has never actually followed his own guide, but we both believe the principles contained within it are a good framework for new players and/or those who are trying to improve their self-discipline.

THE BALANCED MANAGER

The balanced manager takes a little from each different playing style.

We have dealt with five quite polarised playing styles above and, most likely, the majority of consistently successful managers are not too far across any one spectrum. To have the best chance at consistent success, take a little something from each playing style and be prepared to adapt to the nuances of the season. First and foremost, take a look at yourself. How do you like to play the game?

If you are the sort of person who gets your kicks through nailing the big hitter each Gameweek, and you don't mind occasionally being wrong, then don't subscribe to a strategy which locks you into a premium captain for the season. Likewise, if the thought of transferring out a player, only for them to haul, keeps you awake at night, then perhaps a more patient approach is better for you.

FPL is a very personal journey and it is critical that you enjoy it (more on that in the next part). Whichever way you decide to play the game, I believe there is some merit to be taken from each of these playing styles.

The key to my successful campaigns has been when I have taken a balanced approach. I am more risk-averse when I have a good rank, which I want to protect. I take more punts when I've had a poor start and need to catch up. I always aim to keep my first Wildcard intact until Christmas, but I will play it in a heartbeat if I am facing an injury crisis or my team is really not working out for me. I use a combination of both key statistics and watching the games. I have two young children and a full-time job so, of course, I don't watch every match, but if my transfer decision is between Jamie Vardy and Harry Kane, I will watch the Leicester and Spurs games.

I implement my own personal rules to cover the aspects of my style where I know I can succumb to temptation, but I am always prepared to divert from them if I feel that staying on a certain course will be disastrous.

GOLDEN RULE #3:

Be patient in all aspects of FPL but be prepared to adapt, at the right time, when things clearly aren't working out.

Being patient does not mean banging your head against a brick wall for ten solid Gameweeks, when a player you were sure was going to be brilliant just isn't returning for you. Likewise, being adaptive does not mean transferring out a player immediately in exchange for a short-term fix. It is finding that balance between patience and knowing when to act.

I'm afraid this skill isn't one you can learn from a book. It takes time and experience to hone the instinctive gut feeling which guides you either in the direction of perseverance when something isn't working out, or in deciding that this is the perfect time to jump off a particular ship. And trust me: it doesn't matter how long you have been playing the game, you will still get this wrong sometimes.

But being *aware of the need* for that balance will help guide your decisions and lead you down the correct path, more often than not. To give some examples of being patient but adaptive:

Make transfers as late as possible, unless a price change will ruin your plans

As a general principle, make sure you leave your transfers until as late as possible and don't worry too much about price changes. Even if you are 99% certain you have made your decision, gather as much information as you can before committing to the transfer.

However, if you have orchestrated a four-Gameweek transfer plan (and I advocate such forward planning) which is sensitive to a £0.1m price change that you know is imminent, then it may well be worth, in this case, making an early transfer to avoid the price change. This calculated risk is part of being adaptive. Yes, this could backfire; however, *not* acting will definitely ruin a plan which you have carefully plotted. You are adapting to a situation whereby you stand to lose more by being patient than you do by acting right away. As long as you are patient the rest of the time, when there is no obvious benefit to rushing, then there is no problem with occasionally making an early transfer.

Make sure you are patient with long-term strategies but know when it is time to abandon them

Another example would be where you are employing a rule-based strategy such as the "Lock and Swap" one discussed earlier. The effectiveness of such strategies depends on patience because it forces you to stick to your chosen premium players during the low-scoring Gameweeks, so that you can reap the rewards of the high-scoring Gameweeks. However, the high-scoring Gameweeks will not *necessarily* come.

Prior to the 2020/21 season, when the player prices were announced, Pierre-Emerick Aubameyang was reclassified as a midfielder. He had been such an explosive and reliable asset in previous seasons that the prospect of him gaining an extra point per goal and clean sheet left managers salivating. He became a "must have".

After two modest returns in the opening Gameweeks, Aubameyang deteriorated with blank after blank. At some point you have to question the wisdom of continuing down a certain path, even when your own guiding principles insist you do. Where exactly you draw this line is a personal decision, but you need to distinguish between being patient and being foolish.

The difference can be subtle, but listen to your gut and don't make these big decisions when you are angry or feeling negative. Perhaps there are other forces at work which could make this decision an exception?

In the above example, Arsenal were struggling with transition. Mikel Arteta was determined to tighten up the infamous Arsenal defence and did actually make inroads, but at the expense of attacking prowess. The entire team struggled and there was a definite sense this would be, at the very least, a medium-term problem.[28] Again, this comes down to an instinctive sense that something is wrong which overrides your patience and says, "Right, you've stuck with this for long enough; it is time to change it."

Evaluate your own strategies – is the game moving on?

Finally, be patient with yourself. If you have stuck to your own principles, which you firmly believe in, but find yourself languishing in the lower ranks, the temptation to start doubting your own playing style or strategy will creep in. You may well be tempted to change your ways to get out of the situation you are in.

- Perhaps you promised yourself that you would save your Wildcard until a given point in the season but now you want to play it after just three bad Gameweeks.
- Perhaps you told yourself you were going to give the armband to one of your premium assets irrespective of

[28] As it happened, Aubameyang's lack of form was a season-long issue (bar a random hat-trick in GW24) and he appeared a shadow of his former self. In the 2021/22 season, he was released by Arsenal following a spate of disciplinary issues which suggest that the player's attitude was in part responsible for this crash in form.

his fixture, but now you are tempted by another option with a better fixture.

This is a dangerous juncture. If your principles are well reasoned, then you should start to see a change in fortunes if you stick to them. If you succumb to temptation and start changing your own style, or rules, mid-season then you could end up with a double whammy whereby you miss out on the good period which was coming and instead find the new style you have adopted has become the wrong one.

That being said, you must also be willing to adapt. Perhaps you have noticed that, no matter how much you stick to your principles, they do not seem to be working out. Maybe the principles were wrong in the first place and you need to revisit them. Be honest with yourself. Are your principles logically sound? If they are, could it be that the game has moved on from the time you originally set your principles?

The general consensus in the 2017/18 season (and the seasons prior) was that premium defenders were essentially a waste of money. Defenders relied mostly on clean sheets to earn points, and a single goal conceded in a game could wipe that out, no matter how well they played. But the game was moving on.

By 2018, modern strategy, tactical formations and increased player fitness regimens were favouring attacking full backs more than ever. As a result, a number of attacking defenders were regularly scoring more points than their midfield counterparts. Suddenly, the whole concept was turned on its head. Here you had £6m defenders who had higher goal involvement than similarly priced midfield and forward options. On top of this, you could still get the odd clean sheet as well. If your defender scored or assisted and kept a clean sheet, the three bonus points were as good as guaranteed. The value in these players was immense. By 2019/20, many successful FPL managers had a back three or even a back four comprised entirely of attacking full backs.[29]

As FPL managers we have to be able to adapt to the changes within the game and be prepared to rip up the old rule book when new patterns emerge. Walking the tightrope between exercising patience and adapting to the nuances of a season is one of the most powerful things you can master.

***

Irrespective of your playing style, the most important thing is to remember that you are playing a game and that, on balance, it should provide you with enjoyment. FPL is an incredibly psychological game. It is very addictive and can bring immense highs. But it can also send you to some deep lows. I believe there is a positive correlation between enjoying the game and success within the game. It is therefore crucial to master the psychological aspects of being an FPL manager.

[29] Alexander-Arnold, Robertson and Digne anyone?

PART 4:
PSYCHOLOGY

I spent a good few years trying to convince my wife to play FPL. My wife is logical, good with numbers and highly competitive, so I thought FPL could well be something that she would enjoy.

On our trip around the world, she would often need distracting from a difficult hike or 20-hour bus journey, so I would make her recite all the Premier League teams, who got promoted, who got relegated, their players, their manager, the stadium they played at and so on.[30] This would last for hours at a time and went on for the best part of a year. By the end of the 2010/11 season, she could match, or better, any of my football-mad friends for in-depth knowledge of Premier League squads.

When we got back home, I exploited her renewed knowledge of the game and registered her for the 2011/12 season, finally convincing her to set up her own squad.

She got off to a good start in the season and really got a kick out of the big points hauls and outscoring her, at the time, boyfriend (me). But then the inevitable time came when things didn't look so rosy. Tough decisions had to be made. Transfers didn't pay off. Unexpectedly low points returns. Injuries. Wildcard flops. We've all been there.

My wife knows her own mind. She deleted her account and has never returned to FPL since. Her reasons were twofold: first, she didn't get enough positives out of the good Gameweeks to compensate for the pain of the bad ones. Second, she couldn't stand it when a situation arose where FPL conflicted with her as a Liverpool fan – e.g. when she found that part of her did not want Liverpool to score, because she didn't want to lose a clean sheet from an opposition asset she owned.

[30] She's a lucky lady!

The negative effect on her was profound, and this is a person who was not all that passionate about football.

***

I adore FPL. I genuinely love the game and am so glad that it was created. I know it will be a big part of my life until I am so old that I am trying to figure out who can take my team forward in the event of my death. But it is easy to underestimate the psychological impact that it can have on you. Time at home with my family is sacred, yet I have had my entire weekend ruined because my captain blanked in the 8pm Friday night game. I have had disrupted sleep and strange dreams because I've been anxious about a player I don't own or worrying about a decision I have made. It sounds silly, but it is very real and I know I am not alone.

In November 2021 a study exploring the mental health of individuals who play fantasy football was published.[31] While the majority of participants surveyed did not experience mental health concerns, the study found that individuals who engaged the most in fantasy football had significantly worse mental health scores than those who engaged less.

An interesting aspect of the study was that those players with more experience of the game showed the opposite results, and I have found this to be true about myself; the more seasons I have got under my belt, the easier it has been to tolerate the negative aspects of the game. This is because when you enjoy participating in something which has a bad side, you learn to avoid that bad side or develop coping mechanisms for lessening its impact.

---

[31] The study in full can be found here: https://onlinelibrary.wiley.com/doi/full/10.1002/hbe2.316

In this section I will focus on the psychological elements of the game, how to regulate stress and anxiety and how to prevent yourself from making poor decisions because of high-running emotions.

ENJOY IT!

This is one of those annoying things which is very easy to say but not nearly as easy to do, but it is important to enjoy FPL. To do this, you first have to be willing, and able, to accept the negative feelings which follow a bad Gameweek, a poor transfer or wasted Wildcard. These bad feelings pave the way for the positive feelings of a mega points haul, your captain getting an injury-time goal, or a Triple Captain chip which earns you 60 points. If you are not at all frustrated by a poor Gameweek, then you probably won't be delighted by a great Gameweek.

Being a football fan is no different. As a Liverpool fan I have endured some difficult periods in my lifetime. But the feeling of lifting the Champions League trophies in 2005 and 2019, and the end of the thirty-year wait for the Premier League title in 2020, were some of my most treasured moments. Without those bad times[32] the feelings of joy would have been nowhere near as profound.

To tip the scales in favour of positivity, it is important to set expectations of negativity and prepare yourself for it. This is true with many aspects of life.

Be aware of your feelings, if FPL is literally frustrating you to the point where it is causing you to feel grief, anxiety and fear, in particular if it is affecting your relationship with your family, friends or employer, then you should seriously consider stepping back from it.

Mental health comes first.

---

[32] The names Roy Hodgson, Paul Konchesky and Christian Poulsen suddenly spring to mind.

Luck

I will say this again: the single most important factor in FPL success is luck.

I very deliberately pointed this out in the opening chapter of this book. It is crucial that you understand this and have it in the forefront of your mind when trying to regulate your own negative emotions for the game. It is also important for keeping yourself humble when you are having an excellent Gameweek (or season) and are crushing your opponents in a mini-league.

I once heard someone say that playing FPL is like buying 15 raffle tickets. All we are doing, as managers, is making educated guesses at which raffle tickets will be drawn each week. Each ticket has a different probability of winning and a cost associated with that probability. When you play FPL, you have to do so pre-prepared and willing to accept the bad times. Every time a Gameweek goes live, you are rolling the dice or waiting for the raffle to be drawn.

10 TIPS FOR REGULATING NEGATIVE EMOTIONS

Feeling frustrated, angry and jealous are part and parcel of playing FPL. You cannot care about FPL and not experience negativity; it is a physical impossibility. However, there are things I have learned (and often need to remind myself of) which can help keep these negative emotions in check and prevent them from taking over my decision-making processes.[33]

1. Have an FPL routine

Some Gameweeks, particularly over Christmas, make this impossible but, for the most part, I have a pretty solid routine when it comes to how I interact with FPL.

After a Gameweek has finished, I will watch the highlights of the matches on TV to reconcile the results with what can actually be viewed and evaluated. When FPL have finished processing all the data, and the positional tables are totally up to date, I will have a look at my overall rank, type up a report about that Gameweek for my Instagram and Twitter profiles and have a look where I stand against my mini-league opponents. Then, whether I have had a good or a bad Gameweek, I will give it a rest for a couple of days. I go about my normal life and will not *actively* think about FPL. If my mind naturally wanders to it[34] I will allow it, but I do not do any major research or planning.

[33] Or ruining the weekend for my wife and kids!

[34] Which, invariably, it does.

On Wednesday morning, I will start having a big think about what I am going to do in the next Gameweek and form a shortlist of potential transfer options. Sometimes the answer jumps right out at me; other times I know it is going to be a difficult decision which goes right down to the wire. If there are midweek Champions League games on, I keep an eye out for any injuries which may affect my plans and for standout performances which could sway me in a different direction.

Thursday and Friday are my main planning days. With the exception of the Europa League and Premier League press conferences, which can often throw a last-minute spanner in the works, I now have most of the information I need. This is when I consult last week's plan and check if that is still the direction I want to go. This is the stage when I will start looking at statistics, watching replays of the games and checking the upcoming fixtures.

On Friday, I will look out for important information in the press conferences and make sure that nothing has cropped up which would cause me to alter my plans.[35] Please note: at this point I will usually be about 95% certain what my transfer is going to be but, crucially, I have not yet made it!

Late Friday night, just before dinner, I will physically make the transfer and write up a brief report for my social media accounts. There is an argument to say that I should hold off on the transfer until Saturday morning (and during Covid times I do), because players can pull up with an injury beforehand; however, this doesn't happen all that often and it is more

[35] Press conferences are a valuable source of information. As well as being the principal point of learning about last-minute injuries, these conferences can be very revealing in terms of managers' thought processes. Changes to the normal system or squad rotation can often be illuminated here.

important to me to wake up on Saturday morning knowing that the decisions are out of my hands and my fate is with the FPL Gods.

This enables me to instantly spend positive time with my family at the weekend, instead of going back through the almost endless loop of options FPL presents us with. It also prevents me from undoing hours of dedicated thought and research because I have heard some comment about a player on social media which has cast doubt on my decision. Get it done on Friday night and enjoy your weekend.

There is another advantage to this. If, like me, you enjoy a drink (or two) on a Friday evening, then it is sensible to ensure your team and transfers are locked in prior to the consumption of any alcohol. As we know, alcohol lowers our inhibitions and completing transfers whilst under the influence can undo all the self-discipline and logic we have been exercising.

Throughout the weekend, I tend to watch just the Liverpool game live and follow the other games either on the radio or on live text. Sometimes, a family activity will prevent me from checking on this at all, so I will catch up on the result when the game has finished.

Obviously, during the weekend, your mood <u>will</u> be influenced by the goal scorers, assisters, defenders and keepers who have, or haven't, kept clean sheets etc. This is normal and is part of the game. Try not to obsess over it. A bad Gameweek can be turned around by a solid performance from just one player in the last match, so take the information as it comes and try not to predict your own doom too early.

Try not to obsess over your live rank. Websites such www.livefpl.net and www.fantasyfootballfix.com are wonderful and very well put together. They are a great source of information to compare your live rank in real time but, essentially, all that matters is your rank at the end of the Gameweek,[36] so if it is stressing you out, stop looking at it. I'll be honest, I tend to check it when I instinctively feel that I have had a good Gameweek but will deliberately not look at it if I feel the week is going badly. Sometimes, if things are going really badly, I will look at it just to see how bad the damage is so I can adjust my expectations accordingly. I always gauge my own mood before checking my live rank.

When the matches are over, all the results are in, the bonus points are confirmed and the global tables are updated, take a look at how you did and then put FPL away for 24 hours. This is particularly important if you have had a bad Gameweek or are still reeling because your captain's haul was denied by a missed penalty or, as is more the case these days, VAR disallowing a goal from one of your differentials because a particularly curly armpit hair was offside.

It is vital at this stage to give yourself the time to cool down, suppress your emotions and reflect properly on the Gameweek. If you don't, you could be vulnerable to one of the most sinister temptations of all.

2. Don't make rage transfers

A "rage transfer", as it is known in the FPL community, occurs when you make a transfer while you are still raging from something which has happened in the Gameweek. I have even known managers to make rage transfers mid-game, when there are still other matches to be played in that Gameweek.

[36] And ultimately at the end of the season.

Imagine the scene:

You spent all last week deliberating between Player X and Player Y. As is often the case, there is very little between the players and that is why the decision is so difficult. You've looked at the stats, received (no doubt conflicting) advice online and watched highlights of the relevant matches. You change your mind about 12 times and eventually settle on Player Y.

Player Y blanks in the early Saturday match. Player X scores a brace in the first half of the Saturday late match. In the second half, he thumps in a 25-yard volley to complete his hat-trick. This hurts. A lot.

You made totally the wrong decision. You simply *knew* that you should have transferred in Player X instead, yet you didn't! What an idiot you are! Now, following his hat-trick, his price is going to rise as people flock to bring him in. You might even end up missing out again if his price goes up too much. There's only one thing for it. Transfer him in now. Undo your stupid mistake this very instant and swap Player Y for Player X. *Confirm transfers?* Click.

There is so much wrong with the above:

1. The decision didn't work out for you – that does not mean it was a bad decision (more on that later).

2. You didn't *know* that this would happen. You cannot predict the future any more than any other FPL manager out there.

3. You are not an idiot. You thought through your decision, did research, sought advice and, on this occasion, it didn't go your way. The raffle ticket was a dud.

4. His price may go up. So what? That doesn't make transferring him in, right this second, the correct decision. How much money do you have in the bank? He can't rise more than £0.3m in a week anyway.

But you were angry, and you made the transfer anyway. Let's have a look at the situation you are in now:

1. You haven't taken the time to check who Player X and Player Y are playing in the next few Gameweeks – you could have made yet another decision which is going to go against you.
2. The Gameweek has not yet finished. What if one of your other premium assets gets injured? What if another, cheaper player on your watchlist scores a hat-trick? You have now lost the ability to bring that player in (without taking a points hit).
3. Is Player X playing in Europe next week? He could get injured there or have his minutes managed and not feature next week.

Don't get me wrong, your rage transfer *could* work out for you, but if it does, it is only because the 50% luck factor has overridden the other factors. As for the elements you *can* control well, you have just thrown them firmly out of the window. You are now left with just luck and, as we know, that can go either way.

3. Avoid illusions of divination

An often-cited form of angst for FPL managers is what I like to refer to as "illusions of divination". We have all had the following thoughts when making a difficult transfer decision:

"I really want to bring in Player X [who has returned in the last five successive games] but I know he will blank as soon as I bring him in."

"I know I should get rid of Player Y; he has blanked in the last five Gameweeks, and his underlying stats look poor, but I just know that he will haul as soon as I get rid of him."

These feelings are natural and there is no shame in having them, but you have to get a grip of them. You are not God.

The eight million FPL managers out there will not suffer, or benefit, because of your decision. Whether a player blanks (or hauls) has absolutely nothing to do with you. Logical decisions should not be overridden by a fear of bad karma or a sense of cosmic justice working against you.

4. Be wary of fear of missing out (FOMO)

A strange phenomenon in humans is a fear of loss or of missing out. It is why scrapping crowds at Black Friday sales events are such a strange enigma of human behaviour. Why are people driven to flock to crowded shops and literally fight with fellow people over discounted televisions which, in two months' time, are going to be widely available at the same price? It is the fear of missing out which drives people to do this.

That same psychological oddity can influence our decisions in FPL as well. And it can apply in both directions. Holding on tightly to Player X, who is repeatedly under-performing, because you are worried he will haul and reward owners who kept patience, is not a logical reason to keep him. There is a difference between being patient because you are certain the good times will come and being frozen into indecision by fear.

Likewise, getting rid of Player A, who is performing perfectly well, because you need to make room for Player B, who everyone else is suddenly buying in, due to a one-off hat-trick, is not a good reason to make the transaction.

Holding on to Player X, or bringing in Player B, may provide the right *outcome*, but the *decision* will be wrong if it is made due to a fear of missing out. This is an important distinction to make.

5. Dealing with chip fails

These days, I rarely get my Wildcards wrong (after years of learning the hard way how to use them). I do, however, seem to get mixed returns from my other chips. This has been a source of much anguish for me and, as you will have guessed from the fact that I keep mentioning it, I still carry the scar from the great *Mané Triple Captain Fail of 2020*.

It wasn't just the Mané DGW Triple Captain chip which failed me. The season before (2018/19), I used my Triple Captain on Leroy Sane and, again, got three points over two games. The season before, I got six points from Harry Kane. Double what I got in the next two seasons, but still woefully under what you would expect from a premium asset playing twice in a Gameweek. I've actually forgotten what happened in the seasons previous to those I have mentioned, which is a good indication that the returns were underwhelming. Meanwhile, I see people earning 60-point hauls from using the Triple Captain chip on a player in GW1 and getting it just right.

That kind of bad luck can be enough to make you want to change your ways but, when it comes down to it, you cannot ignore the fact that, despite what has happened in previous seasons, playing your Triple Captain on a double Gameweek just *has* to make the most sense. It is why I continue to do it, even though it has worked against me. If this continues to happen, there may come a point where I have to change my ways but, for now, I am willing to write off the past three years as bad luck.

The other point to make is that, while I always tend to play my Wildcard to good effect and mostly seem to get instant gratification (that is to say, a good result on the Gameweek I play it), I see lots of managers who feel that they have wasted their Wildcard because they didn't get the instant points, or rank boost, they were looking for. If you feel like this, remember, you did not play your Wildcard with solely the next Gameweek in mind.

Your Wildcard is a reset button. It is as important as your GW1 set-up. It should be played with the next six Gameweeks factored in. So, if you think you've wasted your Wildcard, then come back in six weeks; I'm sure you will see the fruits of your decisions over the period.

But sometimes, yes, managers *do* waste their chips, and when it happens it is not pleasant. However, as Eric Freeman very wisely points out in his Lock and Swap strategy, for all the agonising we do, for all the time and effort we spend, not to mention the mental anguish we put ourselves through, our chips probably contribute to about 50 points of our final score. And while 50 points is not a negligible amount, our seasons are defined by our weekly transfers and not how we played our chips.

6. Keep it simple

This advice is amongst the most powerful I can offer as it simultaneously improves your chances of FPL success and makes the game more enjoyable to play.

Keep. It. Simple.

If you are trying to decide who to give the captain's armband to, start with your most expensive premium player. Is he in good form? Is he playing against a team with a poor defensive record? If yes, then what is there to get stressed about? Don't allow yourself to get flustered because a mid-priced player put in an excellent performance in the previous Gameweek. The captaincy decision this week is fairly obvious. By all means explore the other options but, more often than not, when all the signs point to one player, that is the one to go for.

You can drill down all you like into stats, systems, formations, tactics and rumours. You may have noticed that Player X cuts inside from the left 67% of the time and that, in the next Gameweek, they are likely to be up against Player Y, who has been vulnerable to left-footed players in 11 out of the last 18 games and even more so in seasons which fall in a leap year (and so on, and so on...) but this level of detail can drive you insane.

If it is getting too much for you, just step back and clear your mind. Is the player in form? Are the fixtures that are coming up reasonable? This is usually a solid basis for any transfer (in) decision. Pair this with the same mentality for your transfer (out) decision. Is the player under-performing? Do they have difficult fixtures coming up? If so, get shut of them. Easy.

I have seen people post things on social media like this:

"This season [Player X] has blanked in every Gameweek after a Gameweek where he has returned. As he hauled last Gameweek, avoid him this Gameweek."

This is meaningless drivel. Do not allow yourself to get sucked in by superstition and end up factoring things like this into your transfer decisions. Just because a pattern has emerged does not mean that pattern is going to continue. If you flip a coin six times and it goes heads, tails, heads, tails, heads, tails, does it mean there is a higher probability that it will be heads next? No, not one bit. There is, and always will be, a 50/50 chance.

Many of the most successful FPL managers out there keep their captaincy and transfer decisions as simple as possible. They also probably sleep better at night.

7. The power of doing nothing at all

As I write this, the wife of one of my friends has an overall rank of 21k in the world, almost a third of the way into the season. She set up her team with a bit of guidance from my friend and made sensible choices. She hasn't touched her team since and is currently beating most of the seasoned FPL veterans I know. I am not for one second advocating a "set and forget" squad. That would (in most cases) be disastrous over an entire season. However, there is a lot to be said for doing nothing at all.

I owe my highest ever rank in part to the situation I was in at the time. Back in 2010 when I was travelling without a smartphone (did smartphones exist back then?), I was reliant purely on internet cafes or the hostels I was staying in having PCs. Mostly, I found I could make my changes each week during my travels but, for a significant part of the season, there were times when I just couldn't do it.

What struck me as odd was the number of times I would come back to civilisation, log onto a PC, check that Gameweek's results and think something like:

"Hmm... he did well, and I definitely would have transferred him out if I had been able to."

There are over eight million registered FPL teams and counting. A lot of these teams are referred to as "ghost teams", which is defined as any team in which there has been no transfer activity at all since it was registered. There are many reasons this could be. More often than not, someone has introduced a friend to FPL and convinced them to set up a team, but real life has got in the way and/or they haven't really taken to it and have never gone back.

There are also many "semi-ghost" teams: people who play FPL but don't take it seriously or perhaps play on and off, sometimes forgetting about it for months on end. We've all got the friend who says to you:

"Oh, I didn't realise there were teams not playing each other last week, did you know that?"

You nod back to them manically, dark circles under your twitching eyes from the weeks of stress which have gone into preparing for the blank Gameweek your friend didn't know about.

Mostly, these "semi-ghost" teams will sink to the middle or bottom of the overall barrel. But not always. In the 2016/17 season a ghost team finished the season with 1,984 points, giving him/her an overall rank of 36,333. No chips played. No Wildcards played. He/she simply set up a decent team and disappeared into the sunset, beating an enormous number of avid FPL managers along the way, including myself.

The point I am trying to make is that, sometimes, doing nothing can be the right decision. I would not advocate it as a long-term strategy but if you ever look at your squad and are struggling with your transfer decision *because* there is no one you want to get rid of, then this is generally a really positive sign. If you really don't want to get rid of someone, then don't. Leave your team how it is. Roll that free transfer over because the same may not be true in the next Gameweek. When in doubt, do nowt.

8. Bad decisions vs bad outcomes

The two are not always the same thing. Just because a decision you made led to a bad outcome (you transferred out a player who hauled, for a player who blanked) does not mean it was a bad decision. The result may not have been favourable; however, the thought process and the logic might have been spot on.

Conversely, just because you raked in the points playing your Triple Captain on Clint Dempsey on the one Gameweek he scored a brace[37] does not mean you are a tactical genius and, importantly, it doesn't make it a good decision. As we have discussed, luck is a huge factor: a bad decision can lead to good results and a good decision can lead to bad results. However, a bad decision will lead to bad results *more often* and vice versa.

Also remember, just because your transfer didn't give you instant gratification does not mean it was a poor one. All of your decisions carry forward into the future. One blank doesn't necessarily imply failure.

9. Prepare for conflicting feelings

If you play FPL, then there's a good chance you really enjoy football (although this is not always the case). If it so happens that you support a Premier League team then, at some point, what you want from your FPL team is going to come into conflict with what you want from real-life football.

[37] A mini-league rival of mine genuinely did this – we don't speak any more.

As a Manchester City fan who owns Bruno Fernandes, you will want, and simultaneously not want, him to score during the Manchester Derby. If you feel this conflict edging its way into your FPL decision-making process, then be wary of it. It is important to be able to make clear, logical decisions and impartiality is essential, especially when there is conflict.

As a Liverpool fan during the defensive injury crisis of the 2020/21 season, I had to acknowledge that teams playing us would be more likely to score. As the season progressed, and our own attacking threat dried up, it became apparent that defenders who played for our opposition were much more likely to get a clean sheet. I didn't like it one bit, but does that mean that I, as an FPL manager (rather than a Liverpool fan), shouldn't consider exploiting the opportunity? Absolutely not.

There will also be conflicts within your squad and in your own head. On many occasions, one of your attacking assets will be up against one of your defensive assets, effectively putting you in a lose–lose situation. I have seen managers bend over backwards with transfers (and sometimes by playing their Free Hit) trying to avoid this happening. Again, you must make the right decisions for the long term. Occasional conflict is inevitable, so take it on the chin and move on.

Finally, we have all been there when our captain has blanked and a player we own, who is highly captained by others, is playing a team with a poor defence next. You can end up with this weird sensation where you are effectively wishing that your own player will blank because you don't want others to benefit more. This is a natural part of the game. Look past these feelings and remember that, while a player may be highly owned at 55%, that means that 45% do not own that player at all, and many that do will be in a rank tier so different from your own that it will have a negligible impact on you. So, try not to wish blanks on your own players; it's not healthy.

10. Avoid early kick-off captaincy

It is important to recognise that this is a recommendation not from a best practice point of view but from a psychological one. I advocate always picking the best captain for each Gameweek, even if that means he is playing in the Friday night kick-off. But doing so is laden with danger from a psychological perspective.

If your captain blanks on a Friday night, it can set a sour mood for the rest of the weekend and you can find that you dread the later matches which involve highly captained players. Those captains may blank themselves but, by that point, the damage is done, the weekend has been tainted.

This comes down to your own personal mental pain threshold. If the captaincy choice is too close to call, I will often go for the later one, but if all arrows point to an asset in the early kick-off, I will grin and bear it. I would rather do the right thing by my FPL team and risk the bad start to my weekend.

If you are really torn because you know deep down that the right captaincy option is playing in the early kick-off and you equally know that him blanking will ruin your weekend, there is an alternative – "The *Match of the Day* Challenge".

This is where you abstain from checking your phone, tablet, laptop, desktop – or any kind of electronic device – all Saturday (or even all weekend, if you can stomach it). The very first time you log into a device will be to watch *Match of the Day*, having no prior knowledge of what has happened.

In September 2021, I went to Geronimo Festival with my wife and kids. We camped at the festival for three nights over the weekend. I was determined not to dampen the experience by being on my phone constantly while the matches were on. So I decided to hide all the apps which could show me what was going on in the world of football. When we got home, I watched *MOTD,* followed immediately by *MOTD2,* and allowed an entire weekend's worth of football action to unfold before my very eyes in the space of two and a half hours.

Don't get me wrong, it was difficult to do and at one point, while I was eating my lunch, I overheard a man telling his friend that Lukaku had scored, which meant I went into the Chelsea game on *MOTD* with some unwanted knowledge. That being said, it was great fun, and it is a clever way of circumventing the early kick-off captaincy dilemma.

SOCIAL MEDIA

As with all aspects of life, social media can be a double-edged sword for FPL.

On the one hand, social media can be a vital source of information, a place where like-minded FPL fanatics get together to share views and opinions, to record their unique FPL journeys with friends. I have seen people post online that the FPL community has been the thing which has got them through tough times in their personal lives.

It can, however, exacerbate problems for those who are already in a bad place. It can be an arena where you are bombarded with so much information that you do not know what to do with it. Some interactions, particularly on Twitter, can turn a little nasty and condescending. You can get slanted views, whereby people make a lot of noise about a good Gameweek but are inconspicuous when they have a bad one. This can begin to distort your perception of how well you are doing compared to others.

When John Stones hit 27 points in DGW19 of the 2020/21 season, I was delighted that I owned him. I was having a very bad week and it was becoming apparent that I had wasted my Bench Boost. John Stones was the one shining light in that Gameweek. A quick scroll through my Twitter feed and suddenly every man and his dog owned John Stones. I felt deflated. My ownership of him was going to count for little because, clearly, everyone else owned him too. But that *wasn't* the case. I discovered afterwards that he was owned by just over 10% of players. Managers who did have him made a huge song and dance about it online, creating the illusion of high ownership.

It is important to be able to navigate social media and advice pages with the same balance as you exercise elsewhere. Scrolling through tweets and squad screenshots can get very noisy and, as you would expect, you will get a lot of contradictory opinions. If you rely too heavily on the advice of others, you will end up just as lost as when you started.

If you are going to follow someone on Twitter or Instagram, make sure they post about all their Gameweeks, good and bad. Do they offer a narrative or commentary justifying their decisions? If so, is their reasoning sound? Is their playing style compatible with yours? If the answer is no, then why are you taking their advice?

Finally, keep an eye on your own conduct on social media. If you are openly critical of others for being smug when they have enjoyed a good Gameweek, make sure you watch the tone of your next post when you are doing well, to ensure you are not being hypocritical.

Beware of social kudos

Everyone loves an underdog story, and it is no different with FPL. If you are part of the online FPL community and/or have a group of friends who are really into the game, then you will undoubtedly share how your Gameweek is going, who you transferred in, and who you put the armband on. The social element of FPL is fantastic but, again, can be laden with danger.

If you set one of the highest owned and highest scoring players as your captain in a Gameweek and he hauls, no-one is going to give you a big pat on the back and say: "well done you", because the move was boring and obvious.

If, however, you picked a differential captain who hauled, you will get lots of social kudos. People will be genuinely pleased for you because you took a chance, and it paid off; people like that. You may well find that if you post it online, it gets lots of attention and is re-tweeted or re-shared.

You may have received low levels of social engagement with your recent posts and have noted the positive reaction to your differential captaincy pick. This is where the addictive nature of social kudos can creep in. Wanting to be rewarded with more social recognition, you may find yourself drawn to the 'David and Goliath' approach to playing FPL, continually going for the underdog instead of the more obvious choices.

If this happens, be wary of it because it can lead down a hard path. As discussed earlier, if you are chasing rank (or someone in your mini-leagues) then a differential captaincy pick may well be the best course of action for you at that moment. Just make sure you are doing it for that reason and not for likes and fist bumps.

Don't be disheartened by a slow start

In the 2021/22 season, at the end of GW12, I saw a post from an FPL account on Twitter which said something along the lines of:

"...if you are ranked 500k or below at this stage of the season, you may as well start making reckless decisions. If you want to catch up, then you aren't going to be able to do it with a template team..."

The implication here was that too much of the season had passed for an FPL manager ranked at 500k to possibly claw their way back by making sensible decisions or having a squad composed of highly owned players. I instinctively felt this was a misinformed view, so I did some checking.

During GW12 of the 2021/22 season, the points gap between Top 10k and Top 500k was 95. With 26 Gameweeks left, a manager at 500k would only need to gain 3.65 points on the safety score[38] each week, between that point and the end of the season. That is far from unattainable.

To put that into some sort of context, you need only look at how my campaign started that season. I got off to a painfully average start. I was stuck in and around 500k for the first ten Gameweeks of the season with little movement in either direction. My arrows (green and red alike) were not significant enough to even mention. I was stagnating, despite playing my Wildcard in GW7.

Then I had two really good Gameweeks. I didn't do anything drastic. No points hits, no chips played, no wild captaincy picks. My fortunes (and the faith I had put in my squad) just came together brilliantly. In just two Gameweeks, I went from 584k to 174k. My team, at the time, was rated 80% template (according to LiveFPL.net).[39]

The FPL community on social media has a habit of amplifying only the good things which have happened to someone's squad. Those who have had a poor Gameweek tend to stay quiet – although not all of them.

---

[38] The score needed to avoid a red arrow at a given point in the Gameweek and at a given overall rank.

[39] At the time of writing (GW29 – 2021/22 season) I am ranked 34k with my Free Hit and Bench Boost chips remaining. A strong comeback is possible if you keep calm and stick to your principles.

This has a dual negative effect for those who are on social media. Let's say you've had a couple of great Gameweeks and enjoyed a really healthy rank boost. You go on social media and find that not only has this happened to lots of other people, but many of them have had an even better rank boost than you have. Suddenly, your achievement seems diluted. What were you even getting excited about? You log out disheartened.

As you can imagine, this is even worse for those who have had a terrible Gameweek and suffered a red arrow. The social media bubble therefore creates the illusion that everyone is doing really well except, of course, for little old you. But this is an illusion. If you've had a bad Gameweek, trust me, there are many, many others who have had a worse one.

Over the course of many Gameweeks, this skewed representation of achievement from others can feed the larger and more dangerous illusion that you are falling *so* far behind that you need to change the way you play to stand any chance of catching up. Most of the time, this is not the case, particularly in the first half of a season.

If you start feeling yourself following this thought process, then take a moment to assess the points gap between where you are now and where you want to be. More often than not, you will be surprised by the answer. Don't be disheartened if you get off to a slow start.

GOLDEN RULE #4:
Everything in moderation, including how much time you spend on FPL.

I have saved this until last because it is the best advice I can give, and if you only take away one thing from this book, I want it to be this. This advice encapsulates everything within FPL, including FPL itself. I also think it is good advice for actual life, but I am certainly not a life coach, nor will I ever be.

Everything in moderation means taking a little from all the different aspects of FPL and bringing them together to guide your short-term decisions and long-term plans. As we've discussed in the Playing Styles part, there is no right or wrong way to play FPL. Each method has its own merits and its own drawbacks. This makes FPL so fantastic to play. It is also what makes it so frustrating. What worked one week won't work another and vice versa.

The skill is to take the very best of everything and weave it into the management of your team:

- Read up on stats but don't *just* rely on them for transfer or captaincy decisions.
- Watch the matches to see if players pass the eye test but don't obsess over watching 90 minutes of every game. Just pick the ones you need to focus on and observe critically.
- Take the occasional points hit, if it is the right thing to do, but don't make a habit of it.
- Don't be afraid to take a punt on a differential, but don't overdo it. If you have a team too full of differentials, you will be heavily penalised when the highly owned players

do better (which often they will; that's why they are highly owned).

- Be patient with the players who you believe in, but are going through an unfortunate spot, but don't be stubborn and stick by a player who is consistently under-performing.
- Research FPL, but don't allow it to consume your life. Remember, you (probably) have a job, family and friends. Don't spend time on FPL to the detriment of those other important aspects of your life.
- Celebrate/mourn the good/bad Gameweeks, but remember to enjoy the football for what it is as well. If your team just won but all you can think about is the fact that your captain blanked, then FPL is tainting the game for you. Back off a little.
- Have a brief scan of social media, as it can be a treasure trove of information, but be wary that too much time spent on there can be bad for your mental health and can affect your enjoyment of the game. Be aware of how social media is making you feel and, if that feeling is predominantly negative, have some downtime from it. The stream of opinions, advice and arguments is endless. You can't (and shouldn't attempt to) read it all. Take what you need from it and turn it off.

I think this section is important for those who really care about FPL, and it has been almost cathartic for me to write. The longer you play FPL, the more intense the emotional investment becomes. Some people have aspirations to make FPL their full-time job, and a few have succeeded. For those people, the stakes are extremely high, particularly if being viewed as an FPL expert is paramount to their chances of success. What I would say to every serious FPL manager out there is remember why you started playing in the first place. For fun.[40]

***

If you have made it this far then you have absorbed the best advice I can offer, and it comes from 18 years of trial and error in my quest for FPL success.

FPL has enhanced my love of football and given me so many memorable moments. The fact that it can turn a game such as Burnley vs Crystal Palace into an absolute highlight of the week is extraordinary. If you are fortunate enough to support a team in the Premier League, then you will naturally be interested in how that team does and the results of the fixtures involving teams you are competing closely with. FPL expands that net of interest much further; suddenly, almost every game is important.

It has also introduced me to a fantastic online community of like-minded geeks and obsessives. I have seen people jumping for joy online because they got over 100 points in a Gameweek without playing a chip. I have seen people going absolutely berserk because they are having a terrible Gameweek and their captain has just missed a penalty. I can literally *feel* their emotions through the screen, because I completely empathise with them.

In this last section, I will extract all the tangible advice out of this book and lay it out in a snappier fashion, starting with pre-

[40] For more detailed literature on the psychological elements of FPL there is a book called *The Mind Game: Gaining a Psychological Edge in Fantasy Premier League* written by Ross Dowsett (AKA FPL Raptor) which I would strongly recommend reading.

season and moving chronologically through until the season's end. This will create a "cheat sheet" of sorts, which will summarise the key points of this book.

SUMMARY

Pre-registration (May – July)

- Create a mental (or physical) list of players who you believe will feature in your squad next season.
- Create a template of price points and cover every position with at least one premium and mid-range figure (in £m), distributing your £100m budget across your squad (and leaving at least £0.5m in the bank).
- Try to enjoy life without FPL.

Pre-season (July – August)

- Get a low ID.
- Check the rules of the game to make sure there are no changes from the previous season.
- Analyse pre-season friendlies to gain insight into possible starting XIs, form, and players who are being played out of position.
- Set up your initial squad, ensuring a distribution of funds for premium players in every position, and leaving at least £0.5m in the bank. Selected players should be first choice for their teams, have a reliable FPL scoring history, and not be injured.
- When choosing players for your starting XI, consider the following:

  - Selecting players who have reasonable fixtures between GWs 1 and 6.
  - Targeting set-piece takers as they are likely to generate more points.
  - Spreading the risk as much as possible; try to avoid doubling up on too many teams in your initial squad and steer clear of triple-ups completely.
  - Don't take chances on unproven players, avoid disgruntled players and do not omit players just because they play for a rival team.

- Have a playing bench; do not worry too much about the third spot but ensure you have players who will start occupying positions 1 and 2.
- Set up your team to play either a 3-4-3 or a 3-5-2 formation.
- Pick a sensible captain (premium option with a good opening fixture).
- Prior to the season starting, watch the press conferences to ensure there are no last-minute injuries or player fitness doubts. Be prepared to adapt if there are.
- If you are not happy with your squad, take a note of your first proper draft and try to justify your changes.

GW1 – GW38 (August – May)

- Spend the first 4–6 Gameweeks getting a feel for how the season is going. Stick to your guns and don't do anything too rash. Spend your transfers putting out fires and ensuring your squad is filled with players who are first choice. Try not to take points hits unless they are absolutely necessary.

- When not putting out fires, use a multitude of sources to inform your transfer decisions (stats, the eye test, bookies' odds, form and fixtures). Remember:
    - BUY – players with good form AND fixtures.
    - KEEP – players who have one of the two.
    - SELL – players who have neither.
- It is good practice to plan your future transfers. Just be prepared to refresh your plans when new information presents itself.
- Around GW6, review your squad:
    - If you have had a disastrous start because you have too many injuries/non-starters to cope with, then think about playing your first Wildcard (WC1). You will now have enough data to make informed choices.
    - If your squad is in good shape and you have had a reasonable start, keep your WC1 to navigate through the blank and double Gameweeks around the Christmas period.
- After GW6, the season will have settled and become easier to predict. This would be the best time to distribute funds away from the bench and into the squad.

- As you approach the busy Christmas schedule, rotation and injuries will become more prevalent. At this stage move back towards having a stronger bench.

- Don't worry too much about your team value; it won't have a significant impact on your season.

- Adjust your playing strategy according to your position. Use the "sword" when trying to chase rank; use the "shield" when trying to protect rank. Remember that focusing your team choices around a mini-league could have a detrimental impact on your overall rank.

- Find out in which Gameweek you will lose your WC1 if you don't play it. Ensure you use it before then. Even if you are happy with your squad, you can use it to make minor adjustments.

- Your chip strategy will be different each season, depending on exactly what happens with the schedule. Start thinking about this ahead of the double (DGW) and blank (BGW) Gameweeks. In general terms, plan to use your chips as follows:

    - **Free Hit (FH)** – To navigate your way through a BGW.

    - **Bench Boost (BB)** – To maximise returns in a DGW, especially effective when used in conjunction with a WC.

    - **Triple Captain (TC)** – To maximise returns in a DGW, especially effective when used on a premium asset, who is in good form and has two desirable fixtures.

- When planning your chip strategy, download a copy of Ben Crellin's FPL Planning Spreadsheet. This is vital for getting the most out of your chips by playing them at the right time.
- Around Christmas and the new year, you will likely (but not always) encounter the first of the BGWs and DGWs. Ensure that there have been no changes which will cause you to adapt your chip strategy.
- If the right opportunity doesn't present itself, save the chips for the second half of the season.
- At the very end of the season, things will get volatile again (particularly if teams have mathematically secured the title, European football, or been relegated). Try to use your chips before this happens.
- Chip strategy is team dependant; be wary of advice from others and do not borrow someone else's ideas. To create your own comprehensive chip strategy, follow these steps:
    - Know the schedule.
    - Eliminate the variables.
    - Determine the critical factors and analyse your team with respect to them.
    - Work out what you would do in each case.
    - Input prediction figures for each scenario.
- If a season is affected by Covid, protect yourself using the following:
    - Information is key; don't make early transfers.

- Do not leave it too late to make your transfers.
- Avoid double/triple-ups.
- Have your C/VC on players from different fixtures.
- Have a strong bench.
- Be wary of rotation/injury prone players.

Psychology (all year round)

- Remember, the most important thing, even more than where you finish, is to enjoy the game.
- Always have in the forefront of your mind that luck is the main factor.
- Be humble in victory; be gracious in defeat. Be kind to yourself when things aren't going well.
- Create an FPL routine and try to stick to it.
- Don't be disheartened by a slow start, you can catch up very quickly as long as you stick to your game plan and stay true to your playing style.
- Do not make decisions out of rage, fear of missing out or because you are worried about karma.
- Use social media with care – it is great for information but can often exacerbate a negative frame of mind. Be mindful of your own conduct on social media; it will get noticed if you are hypocritical or unkind to others.
- If your chips fail, don't worry too much; in isolation, they won't make or break your season.

- If you don't get instant results from your Wildcards, come back and review after six Gameweeks.
- Keep your decisions simple and sensible – often doing nothing is the right answer.
- Prepare for conflicting emotions, which are part and parcel of FPL.
- If you get into a bad place with FPL and it affects relationships with your family, friends or employer, back off it.
- <u>Everything in moderation</u>.

CONCLUSION

In the 2011/12 season, I was working for a franchise of a well-known company which sells very high-end audio/visual equipment. The store I worked in was on the outskirts of Manchester, in a posh area where footballers, from both City and United, rent or buy property. Our store attracted many from the footballing world because of its proximity to their homes and the reputation of the goods we sold.

In my relatively short time there, I met Roberto Mancini (who I impressed[41] with a clip from the film *The Incredibles* on one of our 5.1 systems), Uwe Rosler (who I only spoke to in passing) and Nemanja Vidic (whose two young boys I gave a helium balloon to). But there were two encounters in particular, which really stood out:

The first was on a typical wet Monday morning. My train to work was cancelled, so I had to get the next one. I was late and soaking wet by the time I arrived. When I got to the front door, our sales director was hopping around with nervous excitement.

"Sir Alex Ferguson is in the demo room," he half-whispered, half-shouted to me. "Can you stick the kettle on for him?"

Now, I may be a Liverpool fan, but Sir Alex Ferguson is a monumental character to meet, particularly on a Monday morning when you are soaked to the bone and sweating (because you've literally run all the way from the train station). I tried to get a grip of myself and find the right balance between being polite and nonchalant.

---

41 I think...

Pretending I wasn't utterly star-struck, and focusing all my mental energies on not making a total idiot of myself, I made Sir Alex a cup of tea – a good cup of tea, he told me afterwards – and had a very pleasant interaction with him. He was in great spirits that morning, having thrashed Wolves 5-0 (away) at the weekend. He asked me about myself and who I supported (grumbling, good-naturedly, when I said Liverpool). It was a day I will always remember. But perhaps the most memorable encounter of all was with Emmanuel Adebayor.

One of my first acts upon working for this business was, naturally, to introduce my colleagues to FPL. Our sales director, in particular, really enjoyed it and we spoke at length about the game. Around the same time, Adebayor was in between loan spells with Manchester City and was moving home to London to play for Tottenham Hotspur. After his move, we embarked on a major installation project for him down there and saw a lot of him during the planning and design stage, when he would visit the store to discuss exactly what he wanted from his system.

On one such visit, the conversation turned to football, as it often did. Our sales director pointed over to me and told Adebayor that I had him in my FPL team. I got the impression from the conversation that he didn't really know what FPL was. He came over to me, smiling.

"Let me see, let me see," he said. I looked at him and laughed back nervously, the colour draining from my face. What our sales director didn't know was that I had transferred Adebayor out of my FPL team the previous week due to a dip in his form.

"Show him, Matt, get it up on the screen," our sales director shouted to me across the store. There was no getting out of this one. I stammered out my excuses as I typed in my username and password. Adebayor loomed over me, face full of genuine enthusiasm. My squad loaded up. He wasn't in it. He pointed this out.

I still don't know to this day whether Adebayor has just got an extremely dry and intense sense of humour, but he gave the distinct impression that he was genuinely annoyed that I had got rid of him. I cobbled together some excuse that I had heard reports he was injured and had transferred him out, just in case. I assured him that I would put him back in the squad at the next possible opportunity[42] and then tried to change the subject, but the damage was done. He left the shop looking disparagingly at me over his shoulder as he went.

It is the first, and, I hope, only time I have ever had to justify a transfer decision to the footballer himself.

***

I hope that you have enjoyed reading this book as much as I have enjoyed writing it. I stressed early on that luck was a major factor in both FPL success and defeat. I also stated that there are many routes to FPL success, which is why the game is so enjoyable for a wide range of people, with diverse playing styles and football opinions.

It can be an incredibly frustrating game, because predicting the future is not a straightforward task. What works one week can let you down the next. A successful strategy in one season can be a complete flop the next. But what keeps me going is how quickly you can turn your own fortunes around in the course of a season.

It hit me that an FPL season is like a stretched-out version of playing Super Mario Kart. If you have never played Super Mario

[42] I didn't. My FPL squad comes first. My career, second.

Kart, it is great fun but it can be incredibly frustrating. You can go from being first to eighth (last) in a second. But conversely, if you stick at it, you can grind your way back through the ranks quickly.[43]

All we can do as FPL managers is try to tip the scales of luck in our favour and, in doing so, ensure we are staying true to our individual playing style. Often FPL is about getting the basics right and having the self-discipline to keep making sensible choices. When I have been enduring a terrible season, I have often felt myself mentally throwing the toys out of the pram. I've started doing crazy, out-of-character things and making wild decisions. I see other people doing this all the time. Every now and then one of these "rage decisions" comes off but, mostly, we are punished for not staying true to our style and making calm, rational decisions.

An FPL season is like a roller coaster. A squad which earned you 100+ points in GW10 can get you 35 points in GW11. We cannot control what the players do on the pitch but we can control our own decision-making. Self-discipline and patience are key to a successful campaign, but enjoying FPL is the most important thing of all.

[43] Especially if you get one of those spiky blue shells.

RESOURCES

There are countless amazing resources out there which can help FPL managers improve their game, make informed decisions more efficiently, and compile raw data in a more accessible way. Below is a list of the tools I use for FPL:

livefpl.net

This website was primarily conceived as a way for FPL managers to check their live rank in real time. It even processes live rank "post-autosubs" which gives you a more realistic view of where your rank will stand once substitutions have been accounted for. In addition to checking live rank, I use it primarily for investigating ownership at various tiers. Ragabolly (who created it) has packed it with many amazing features. Check it out.

fantasyfootballfix.com (FFFix)

I use FotMob to check on live scores when I am not watching or listening to a match. In tandem, I also consult FFFix's Gameweek Live section because their live statistics feed is customised to your squad and so highlights the things which affect you. To give an example, if a team loses a clean sheet, all the defensive assets related to that team will be shown as losing a clean sheet. It highlights any you own in red.

It also shows who FPL awarded the assist to, which, as we know, can often differ from who the assist was officially awarded to. I find this useful because it helps manage your own expectations (nothing worse than false hope being dashed!). I also use their Price Change Predictor, which tells you which players are going to be hit by an overnight price rise or drop.

As with livefpl.net, it also calculates your live rank. It is jam-packed with other features too. The website and UI are so slick and pleasant to use. They also have an app for Android phones.

fantasyfootballscout.co.uk / fantasyfootballhub.co.uk

These are the two largest websites for all things FPL related. I have been a paying member of both and, for me, it is too close to call between the two. Both websites have a fixture/season ticker, which is important for transfer planning. They also have Opta stats filtered by Key Stats for FPL. I use both a lot.

There are also tons of well-written articles from high-profile FPL managers with good credentials. At the time of writing, the rough cost of a membership is £2 per month for a basic subscription, although you can sign up for less if you pay up front before the season begins.

thefplway.com

This is a relatively new website which offers much of what the previous two websites do but the content is not fee restricted. They have a weekly captaincy article and a number of ad hoc blogs written by prominent members of the FPL community. They also have a brilliant transfer planner which allows you to see what your team will look like in future Gameweeks. It is really slick and great to use.

Live FPL Tables (livefpltables.com)

This is a cracking website for tracking your mini-leagues and checking your league position in real time. Besides what you would expect from the FPL website, it also shows which of your rivals have played a chip, taken a points hit, and how many players they have left to play in the week, all in one place. The UI is super sleek and intuitive. I love it. Highly recommended.

fbref.com

This website is an incredibly comprehensive source of football statistics. It is also home to my favourite stat (NPxG+xA/90) and is totally free to use. It takes a bit of time to work out how to filter the information you want but it's worth it once you've done it.

FPL Away Kits (Google Chrome Extension)

This is a great bit of fun. Quickly install this Chrome extension et voila! All your players who are playing away in the upcoming Gameweek will be shown in their away kit (in the Pick Team tab). Genius!

Pen and paper

When I have some planning to do, there is nothing better than getting a scrap piece of paper and a pen and just getting some thoughts down. Often, all you require is the information which can be gathered from the FPL website and your own brain. My starting point is often jotting down the things which are hovering around my mind and moving on from there.

Sometimes it's good to print off your squad and cover it in handwritten notes, highlighting the players who are likely to make way and potential replacements for them.

ACKNOWLEDGEMENTS

This book is the first piece of non-fiction I have written. There are many people who have guided me along the way, to whom I owe my thanks.

First, I'd like to thank my wife, Rachael, who is my first port of call for bouncing around ideas. My wife is a busy person but always takes the time to listen to me waffle about FPL. She also reads all my work prior to publication and, importantly, tells me what she thinks, rather than what I want to hear. She knows my FPL playing style and keeps me in line when I deviate from it.

I would also like to thank my editor, Ian Howe, who made the process of editing this book (which, frankly, I was dreading) so enjoyable. Ian knows a lot about football but practically nothing about FPL, which turned out to be the perfect combination. While the content of the book was not totally alien to him, he was removed enough from the terminology to know when the language I was using was going down an "FPL-centric" rabbit hole.

I would like to give special thanks to my good friend, Dan O'Reilly, for beta-reading this book and giving me really detailed feedback, despite me saying "I hate him" in it, and for providing me with years of exciting mini-league rivalry. I look forward to many more decades of it.

Thanks also to Pat Best, who not only introduced me to the game in the first place, but gave my final draft a once over (in record time!) and came back immediately with feedback.

FPL COMMUNITY

I have many 'real life' friends who enjoy FPL but, even amongst the most devout players of the game, I have always felt as though my obsession with the game was on another level. Quite often I would be enthusiastically discussing FPL with a group of friends and then note the point at which they started to switch off or move the conversation on. In some regards it felt rather lonely. That was until I discovered the online FPL community.

I started out by creating a dedicated account on Instagram (@fpl_obsessed) and posting screenshots of my squad to, quite literally, no-one. Eventually I got a handful of followers. I started accompanying my screenshots with text, offering reasoning for my weekly decisions. My following started to grow, slowly but steadily.

Then I joined Twitter. An intimidating and strange place for the newly initiated but an absolute mine of useful information and, more importantly, a micro-community of some of the most passionate, obsessive and dedicated FPL managers you could ever hope to meet. I was in heaven. Finally, I could converse with thousands of like-minded FPL enthusiasts and not feel like I was in some way unusual in my love of the game.

As I said in the Psychology section, social media certainly has its downsides and you must be wary of them. But I would advise everyone to create a dedicated account on Twitter and just start interacting with members of the FPL community. If you can safeguard yourself against the dangers, then you will not regret it.

GLOSSARY OF TERMS

Attacking Returns – Usually used in reference to a Defender, attacking returns are points generated from a goal or an assist.

Auto-Substitute – If one of your players plays 0 minutes in a Gameweek, the player on your bench, who is numerically first, will be automatically swapped into your starting XI, as long as this does not lead to an invalid formation.

Bandwagon – Occurs when lots of managers transfer in a player, usually one who was not previously highly owned.

Bench Boost (BB) – One of the four special chips which a manager can play in a Gameweek of their choosing. The Bench Boost allows the points scored by all four bench players to count towards the Gameweek total.

Blank – When a player scores two points or less in a single game. Many consider 3 points to be a blank.

Blank Gameweek (BGW) – Any Gameweek in which there are fewer than ten scheduled fixtures. Players from the teams who are not playing will get 0 points.

Bonus Points System (BPS) – BPS is used to track and reward the players' involvement in the game. Players will accumulate BPS points during the game and, at the end of every game, Bonus Points are given out. Typically, the three best-performing players from each match will receive BPs (3, 2, 1).

Captain (C) – The player who you select as your captain will get double the points in that Gameweek.

Chips – Chips can be used to (potentially) enhance your team's performance during the season. Only one chip can be used in a single Gameweek.

Clean Sheet (CS) – A clean sheet is awarded to a goalkeeper, defender or midfielder when the team they play for does not concede a goal, so long as they played for at least 60 minutes. Any players substituted after 60 minutes will still receive a Clean Sheet, even if their team goes on to concede a goal.

Differential – A differential is a low-owned player, be that in overall FPL terms or in the context of a mini-league. There is no universal definition of what constitutes a differential; however, it is widely considered than any player with less than 10% ownership is a differential.

Double-Digit Haul – When a player accrues ten or more points in a single game.

Double Gameweek (DGW) – Any Gameweek in which there are over ten scheduled fixtures. Players from the teams who are playing twice will have their points from both matches combined.

Doubling up – When you have two players from the same team in your squad.

Draft – Draft is a different way to play FPL, where each player can only be owned once in the league.

Effective Ownership (EO) - Percentage of managers who started a player + percentage of managers who captained that player + percentage of managers who triple captained that player – percentage of managers who benched that player.

Enabler(s) – The cheapest available players (£4m goalkeeper and defender, £4.5m midfielder and forward), who enable you to afford higher-value players elsewhere. These players usually sit on the bench.

Essential / Must Have – A player who, in someone's opinion, is crucial to success either in a single Gameweek or over the course of a season.

Expected Assists (xA) – A metric used to identify the likelihood a given pass will become a goal assist.

Expected Goal Involvement (xGI) – A metric used to track players' expected contributions to both goals and assists.

Expected Goals (xG) – A metric used to identify the likelihood a shot will result in a goal.

FPL Assist – When FPL award an assist, even if the assist is not being officially awarded in the match.

FPL Cup – The FPL Cup starts midway through the season. Approximately half of the existing managers are automatically eliminated (if their rank is in the bottom half overall), and the remaining managers are pitted against each other in a knockout format; the winner advances to the next round. This happens all the way until GW38, where the last two managers will contest the final.

Free Hit (FH) – One of the four special chips which a manager can play in a Gameweek of their choosing. The Free Hit allows the manager to make unlimited free transfers to their squad for that Gameweek. Unlike the Wildcard (WC), the team will revert back to how it was in the Gameweek prior to the chip being played.

Free Transfers (FTs) – Transfer(s) which a manager can make ahead of the next Gameweek which will not incur a points reduction.

Gameweek (GW) – Defined as the period of time 90 minutes prior to the kick-off of the first match and up until the beginning of the next Gameweek.

Haul – When a player makes more than one return in a single game.

Head-To-Head (H2H) – The two different ways of scoring in the game, either the classic scoring, where points are accumulated, or the H2H scoring, where each week a manager is paired with an opponent in the league. The winner takes three points, draw is one point a piece and zero points for a loss.

Hits (Points Hits) – When a transfer is made, once the Free Transfer has been used. This transfer will come with a four-point deduction from the next Gameweek score.

Points hits are therefore in multiples of four (–4, –8, –12 and so on).

In The Bank (ITB) – The amount of money which is surplus to the budget invested in the 15-man squad.

In The Know (ITK) – People who have connections with the Premier League clubs and are therefore privy to confidential information (such as starting XIs and injury news).

Kneejerk – Reacting to a situation quickly and without due consideration.

Mini-Leagues (MLs) – Leagues which you set up with your friends.

Nailed (on) – A player who is expected to start a match as long as they are not injured.

Non-Penalty Expected Goals (NPxG) – Expected Goals (xG) excluding those from penalties.

Out Of Position (OOP) – Usually in reference to a player whose position has been incorrectly categorised within FPL. Example: John Lundstram was categorised as a Defender in FPL but was playing in midfield for Sheffield United in the 2019/20 season.

Overall Points (OP) – The total sum of points your team has accumulated at any point in the season.

Overall Rank (OR) – The rank/position of your team within FPL's Overall Public League at any given time. This is the league which every registered team is automatically included in.

Over-performing – When a player's actual goal involvement is higher than their xGI.

Points Per Game (PPG) – The average number of points a player returns in a Gameweek (Total Points / Number of Games Played).

Points Per Game Per Million (PPG/M) – A ratio of Points Per Game against the cost of the player (used to ascertain a player's value).

Premium/Heavy Hitter – A player who is in the upper price bracket of any given position. There is no approved definition of what the price brackets are but, generally: Defender = £6m+, Midfielder/Forward = £10m+.

Pressers – Premier League press conferences.

Punt – Usually used in reference to a risky or differential transfer.

Rage Transfer – When a transfer is made by somebody who is still angry about something which has taken place in the Gameweek.

Red Card (RC) – When a player is sent off (three points are deducted).

Return – When a player earns any number of points in a single game, besides the two points obtained for playing over 60 minutes. Many consider four points to be necessary to constitute a return.

Squad Value (SV) – The value of your 15-man squad net of money In The Bank (ITB).

Starting XI – The eleven players which form your squad who are not on the bench. Only your starting XI can generate points (unless a Bench Boost has been played).

Template – A hypothetical team comprising the most highly owned players.

Triple Captain (TC) – One of the four chips which a manager can play in a Gameweek of their choosing. The Triple Captain multiplies the selected captain's Gameweek points by three instead of two.

Tripling up – When you have three players (the maximum permitted) from the same team in your squad.

Underlying Stats – An umbrella term for any statistics which evaluate a player's performance but are not as obvious as Goals, Assists, Clean Sheets, Points, etc.

Under-performing – When a player's actual goal involvement is lower than their xGI.

Vice-Captain (VC) – The player selected to become your Captain (C) in the event that your Captain plays 0 minutes in that Gameweek.

Wildcard (WC) – One of the four chips which a manager can play in a Gameweek of their choosing. When the Wildcard is activated, managers can make unlimited free transfers in that Gameweek only.

Wildcard 1 (WC1) – WC1 can be played in the first half of the season. It will be lost if it is not played prior to the designated Gameweek.

Wildcard 2 (WC2) – WC2 can be played in the second half of the season. It will be lost if it is not played prior to GW38.

Yellow Card (YC) – When a player is booked (1 point is deducted).

LEAVING A REVIEW

If you enjoyed this book then please leave a customer review on either Amazon or Goodreads.

As a new author, customer reviews are a vital source of feedback from my readers. They also help others, who are considering reading the book, to have the confidence to make the purchase. Sadly, less than 10% of readers actually go on to leave a review on a book.

If you have five minutes to spare, please give me your genuine thoughts on the book. If you are pushed for time, feel free to drop a one-liner letting me know what you think of the book.

Your reviews will be greatly appreciated.

If you have any feedback you would like to give direct to me, you can contact me on:

Twitter: twitter.com/fpl_obsessed

Instagram: www.instagram.com/fpl_obsessed

ABOUT THE AUTHOR

Matt Whelan lives in Chester, North West England and is the author of a series of children's books called *Adventure Quest*.

While his father nurtured his love of the fantasy and science fiction genres, it was Matt's uncle, Steve, who introduced him to Liverpool Football Club and a lifelong love of football.

In 2004, Matt was introduced to Fantasy Premier League (FPL) which broadened his enjoyment of football beyond Liverpool's matches. He has been an FPL enthusiast ever since.

In 2019, he started creating FPL content on Instagram under the alias, FPL Obsessed. He is now an active member of the FPL community on both Instagram and Twitter.

When not writing - or choosing his captain - he can be found spending time with his wife and two young children or throwing a ball for his dog Neo.